Wise Men Talking Series

YAN ZI
晏子说
Says

蔡希勤 编注

□ 责任编辑 **陆瑜**
□ 翻译 **薛彧威**
□ 绘图 **李士伋**

老人家说
系列丛书

华语教学出版社
SINOLINGUA

First Edition 2012

ISBN 978-7-5138-0158-4
Copyright 2012 by Sinolingua
Published by Sinolingua
24 Baiwanzhuang Road, Beijing 100037, China
Tel: (86)10- 68320585   68997826
Fax: (86)10- 68997826   68326333
http://www.sinolingua.com.cn
E-mail: hyjx@sinolingua.com.cn
Printed by Beijing Songyuan Printing Co., Ltd.

Printed in the People's Republic of China

老人家说

Wise Men Talking

俗曰:"不听老人言,吃亏在眼前。"

老人家走的路多,吃的饭多,看的书多,经的事多,享的福多,受的罪多,可谓见多识广,有丰富的生活经验,老人家说的话多是经验之谈,后生小子不可不听也。

在中国历史上,春秋战国时期是中国古代思想高度发展的时期,那个时候诸子并起,百家争鸣,出现了很多"子"字辈的老人家,他们有道家、儒家、墨家、名家、法家、兵家、阴阳家,多不胜数,车载斗量,一时星河灿烂。

后来各家各派的代表曾先后聚集于齐国稷下学官。齐宣王是个开明的诸侯王,因纳无盐丑女钟离春为后而名声大噪。他对各国来讲学的专家学者不问来路一律管吃管住,给予政府津贴。对愿留下来做官的,授之以客卿,造巨室,付万钟;对不愿做官的,也给予"不治事而议论"之特殊待遇。果然这些人各为其主,各为其派,百家争鸣,百花齐放,设坛辩论,著书立说:有的说仁,有的说义,有的说无为,有的说逍遥,有的说非攻,有的说谋攻,有的说性善,有的说性恶,有的说亲非亲,有的说马非马,知彼知已,仁者无敌……留下了很多光辉灿烂的学术经典。

可惜好景不长,秦始皇时丞相李斯递话说"焚书坑儒",结果除秦记、医药、卜筮、种树书外,民间所藏诗、书及百家典籍均被一把火烧个精光。到西汉武帝时,董仲舒又上书提出"罢黜百家,独尊儒术",从此,儒学成了正统,"黄老、刑名百家之言"成为邪说。

"有德者必有言",儒学以外的各家各派虽屡被扫荡,却不断变换着生存方式以求不灭,并为我们保存下了十分丰富的经典著作。在这些经典里,先哲们留下了很多充满智慧和哲理的、至今仍然熠熠发光的至理名言,我们将这些各家各派的老人家的"金玉良言"编辑成这套《老人家说》丛书,加以注释并译成英文,采取汉英对照方式出版,以飨海内外有心有意于中国传统文化的广大读者。

As the saying goes, "If an old dog barks, he gives counsel."

Old men, who walk more roads, eat more rice, read more books, have more experiences, enjoy more happiness, and endure more sufferings, are experienced and knowledgeable, with rich life experience. Thus, what they say is mostly wise counsel, and young people should listen to them.

The Spring and Autumn (770-476 BC) and Warring States (475-221 BC) periods of Chinese history were a golden age for ancient Chinese thought. In those periods, various schools of thought, together with many sages whose names bore the honorific suffix "Zi," emerged and contended, including the Taoist school, Confucian school, Mohist school, school of Logicians, Legalist school, Military school and Yin-Yang school. Numerous and well known, these schools of thought were as brilliant as the Milky Way.

Later representatives of these schools of thought flocked to the Jixia Academy of the State of Qi. Duke Xuan of Qi was an enlightened ruler, famous for making an ugly but brilliant woman his wife. The duke provided board and lodging, as well as government subsidies for experts and scholars coming to give lectures, and never inquired about their backgrounds. For those willing to hold official positions, the duke appointed them guest officials, built mansions for them and paid them high salaries. Those unwilling to take up official posts were kept on as advisors. This was an era when "one hundred schools of thought contended and a hundred flowers blossomed." The scholars debated in forums, and wrote books to expound their doctrines: Some preached benevolence; some, righteousness; some, inaction; some, absolute freedom; some, aversion to offensive war; some, attack by stratagem; some, the goodness of man's nature; some, the evil nature of man. Some said that relatives were not relatives; some said that horses were not horses; some urged the importance of knowing oneself and one's enemy; some said that benevolence knew no enemy .... And they left behind many splendid classic works of scholarship.

Unfortunately, this situation did not last long. When Qin Shihuang (reigned 221–210 BC) united all the states of China, and ruled as the First Emperor, his prime minister, Li Si, ordered that all books except those on medicine, fortune telling and tree planting be burned. So, all poetry collections and the classics of the various schools of thought were destroyed. Emperor Wu (reigned 140–88 BC) of the Western Han Dynasty made Confucianism the orthodox doctrine of the state, while other schools of thought, including the Taoist and Legalist schools, were deemed heretical.

These other schools, however, managed to survive, and an abundance of their classical works have been handed down to us. These classical works contain many wise sayings and profound insights into philosophical theory which are still worthy of study today. We have compiled these nuggets of wisdom uttered by old men of the various ancient schools of thought into this series Wise Men Talking, and added explanatory notes and English translation for the benefit of both Chinese and overseas readers fond of traditional Chinese culture.

目录

A

B

The administrative ruler cannot enhance his prestige among other states if he is too stubborn to take advice and despises people of benevolence.

不劫人以兵甲，不威人以众强〔10〕

A man who does not coerce the people of other states with military force, or intimidate them with strength in numbers ...

不权居以为行，不称位以为忠〔12〕

A man should not base his own code of conduct on his status; nor decide his necessary degree of loyalty according to his own position.

不掩君过，谏乎前，不华乎外〔14〕

One should reveal a monarch's mistake by offering advice in his presence but not propagating it.

不以饮食之辟害民之财〔16〕

A monarch should not squander people's wealth owing to his own indulgence in food and drink.

不因喜以加赏，不因怒以加罚〔18〕

A wise monarch must not raise rewards for his personal pleasure, nor increase punishments because of private vendettas.

C

臣有德，益禄；无德，退禄〔20〕

If a government official is virtuous, increase his salary; if he is not, decrease it.

朝居严则下无言〔22〕

When the monarch wears a forbidding look at court, his subjects will not dare to speak the truth.

春省耕而补不足者谓之游〔24〕

Examining crop cultivations in spring and offering help to those in need, this inspection tour of the past monarchs is called "yóu".

从高历时而不反谓之流，从下而不反谓之连〔26〕

Indulging in visits to mountain scenery and not thinking of returning is called "liú"; indulging in visits to water scenery and not thinking of returning is called "lián".

寸之管，无当，天下不能足之以粟〔28〕

A bottomless bamboo pipe, short as one *cun*, can never be filled with grain though all the grain in the world be put inside it.

D

德薄而禄厚，智惛而家富，是彰污而逆教也〔30〕

It is an act of condoning corruption which goes against the sages' teachings to have someone lacking in virtue enjoy a high salary or someone injudicious live in plenty.

德不足以怀人，政不足以惠民〔32〕

If the ruler fails to get his people to cherish his morals and to have his politics benefit his people ...

德厚而受禄，德薄则辞禄〔34〕

When one has morals and virtuous conduct, they should receive a salary; when one lacks morals and virtuous conduct, they should return it.

德行教诲加于诸侯，慈爱利泽加于百姓〔36〕

Influencing other states by virtue and morality, treating the people with affection and kindness ...

地不同生，人不同能〔38〕

Like lands are of different properties, people are of different abilities.

F

夫社，束木而涂之，鼠因往托焉〔40〕

Rats find a safe place to live in the altar which is built by binding the wood and then applying mud on it.

富而不骄者，未尝闻之〔42〕

To lead an abundant life yet not domineering, such a man has never been heard of.

G

古之王者，德厚足以安世〔44〕

Those who proclaimed themselves kings in ancient times all had virtues that guaranteed social stability.

古之贤君，饱而知人之饥〔46〕

The wise monarchs in ancient times knew there were common people who were hungry while they themselves were full.

古者先君之干福也，政必合乎民〔48〕

In ancient times, the monarch could pray for blessings only when his policies followed the people's hearts.

古之饮酒也，足以通气合好而已矣〔50〕

The function of drinking in ancient times was only to invigorate blood circulation and entertain guests.

观之以其游，说之以其行〔52〕

We should judge a man by observing his friends and his behaviors.

棺椁衣衾，不以害生养〔54〕

The cost of a coffin and funeral clothes should not be too high, in case it becomes a burden on the living.

贵不凌贱，富不傲贫〔56〕

The nobles should not insult the commoners, the rich should not

5

be arrogant in front of the poor.

贵戚不荐善，逼迩不引过〔58〕

If important ministers do not give good counsel and officials
close to the monarch do not point out his mistakes ...

国有道，即顺命〔60〕

If policies are virtuous and beneficial for the country, then they
must be carried out.

国有三不祥〔62〕

A country has three evil omens.

H

合升斗之微，以满仓禀〔64〕

A full granary begins with a single *sheng*.

J

见善必通，不私其利〔66〕

Officials should implement good policies immediately without
intending to seek personal gain.

见贤不留，使能不怠〔68〕

The monarch should employ the virtuous and capable as soon as
they are found, and after employing them should never neglect
them.

见贤而进之，不同君所欲〔70〕

Virtuous and capable people must be promoted, even if the monarch disagrees with their advancement.

禁之以制，而身不先行，民不能止〔72〕

If the administration wishes to impose bans, they themselves must follow them first. Otherwise, it will be impossible to convince the common men to obey them.

尽智导民而不伐焉〔74〕

The wise monarchs in ancient times tried their best to guide their people to goodness, and did not boast of their achievement.

进不失廉，退不失行〔76〕

Officers should be free of corruption when holding their position and keep their upright characters after withdrawal from their position.

俭于藉敛，节于货财〔78〕

Levying taxes should be moderate, the use of property should be frugal.

节欲则民富，中听则民安〔80〕

If the administrative rulers moderate their desires, the people will be rich. If lawsuits are carried out fairly, the people will live in harmony.

近臣默，远臣喑，众口铄金〔82〕

When the ministers in the court keep their mouths shut and the ministers out of court pretend to be dumb, the criticism from the people could melt even metal.

橘生淮南则为橘，生于淮北则为枳〔84〕

The orange growing in the south was sweet, but that in the north was sour.

举贤以临国，官能以敕民，则其道也〔86〕

The best way to administer a country is to employ the virtuous and capable.

举之以语，考之以事〔88〕

A man should be recommended according to his words, and assessed according to his deeds.

君国者不乐民之哀〔90〕

The ruler or of a country should not base his happiness on the pain of his people.

君屈民财者不得其利〔92〕

The monarch who exhausts the property of the nation cannot achieve personal gain.

君人者与其请于人，不如请于己也〔94〕

If the monarchs want their descendants to succeed them to the throne, it is better to ask help from themselves than from others.

君正臣从谓之顺 〔96〕

The minister who obeys the right order of the monarch is a faithful minister.

君子不怀暴君之禄 〔98〕

Gentlemen do not covet rewards offered by tyrants.

君子独立不惭于影 〔100〕

A gentleman does not feel shame when he stands alone in front of his shadow.

君子居必择居，游必就士 〔102〕

If a gentleman wishes to find a living place, he must make a good choice in his neighbors; when he embarks upon a journey, he must find someone virtuous and talented as his company.

君子无礼，是庶人也 〔104〕

If a ruler or a man of virtue does not pay attention to etiquette, he is no different from the common man.

君子有力于民则进爵禄，不辞富贵 〔106〕

If a gentleman can serve the people, he can take office and enjoy a wealthy life of ease.

君子之事君也，进不失忠，退不失行 〔108〕

If a gentleman serves his monarch, he should maintain his loyalty to his position and keep his upright character when not in office.

L

乐贤而哀不肖，守国之本也〔110〕

Loving the virtuous and capable persons and being sympathetic to the common people is the foundation of governing a country.

礼者，所以御民也；辔者，所以御马也〔112〕

Etiquette is used to govern the people as the rein is used to tame the horse.

廉者，政之本也〔114〕

Being honest and free from corruption is the foundation of good political governance.

M

明君居上，寡其官而多其行，拙于文而工于事〔116〕

Wise monarchs do not create too many positions, they expect their officials to work with high efficiency. They do not pursue ornate appearances, but are practical and unpretentious in all their actions.

明君居上，无忠而不信，无信而不忠者〔118〕

The ministers who are trusted by a wise monarch are faithful, and those who are not trusted are not faithful.

明王不徒立，百姓不虚至〔120〕

No one can easily become a wise monarch; it is impossible for the people to submit to one who governs them without being given any reason to support him.

明王之任人，谄谀不迩乎左右〔122〕

A wise monarch will not let flatterers accompany him.

N

能爱邦内之民者，能服境外之不善〔124〕

The monarch who loves the people in his kingdom has the power to win over the villains of other kingdoms.

Q

其在朝，君语及之，即危言〔126〕

While serving the court, Yan Zi would always reply to the king's enquiries seriously and honestly.

其政任贤，其行爱民〔128〕

The wise monarch employs virtuous and capable persons, cares for the people of his kingdom.

轻死以行礼谓之勇〔130〕

It takes boldness to continue with etiquette regardless of danger.

R

任大臣无多责焉，使迩臣无求壁焉〔132〕

If the monarch does not demand perfection when appointing ministers, does not choose his favorites to be close advisers ...

任人之长，不强其短〔134〕

If we want to utilize someone's merits, we should discount his demerits.

S

上离德行，民轻赏罚〔136〕

If the monarch does not follow moral standards, the people will belittle both the rewards and punishments he metes out.

上无骄行，下无谄德〔138〕

The monarch has no arrogant behaviors, and courtiers are free from flattery.

赏无功谓之乱，罪不知谓之虐〔140〕

Granting rewards to a person who has made no contribution to the nation is called an interruption of administration. Penalizing a person who didn't know the truth of what they had done is called an act of tyranny.

圣人千虑，必有一失；愚人千虑，必有一得〔142〕

Even a wise man may sometimes make a mistake; even a fool may sometimes have a good idea.

食鱼无反，毋尽民力乎〔144〕
Not trying to exhaust the manpower is just like eating one side of a fish without turning it over.

疏者有罪，戚者治之〔146〕
If those who are close are assigned to punish the distant who commit crimes ...

四海之内，社稷之中，粒食之民，一意同欲〔148〕
When all men unite and work as one ...

遂欲满求，不顾细民，非存之道也〔150〕
For a monarch to constantly try to satisfy his personal desires regardless of the lives of the common people is not the right way to govern a country.

所谓和者，君甘则臣酸〔152〕
We can take the flavors as an illustrative example of the relationship between the monarch and his courtiers. If the monarch is sweet, his courtiers should be sour.

T

太山之高，非一石也〔154〕

Just as the Mt. Tai was not formed by one stone ...

天地四时，和而不失〔156〕

Just as the heaven, the earth, the ying and yang, and the four
seasons rotate harmoniously and accurately ...

通人不华，穷民不怨〔158〕

(The country is healthy) when the noblemen are not luxurious
and the poor have no complaints.

通则视其所举〔160〕

The way to judge a man is to watch whom he recommends when
his official career prospers.

W

为臣比周以求进，逾职业防下隐利而求多〔162〕

If courtiers collude for their promotions, overstep their authority,
press hard on the people, seek personal gains insatiably ...

为地战者，不能成其王〔164〕

He who only fights for territory could never become a ruler.

为君厚藉敛而托之为民〔166〕

If the monarch were to increase the taxes and claim it was for
the good of the people ...

为君节养其余以顾民，则君尊而民安〔168〕

If the monarch himself is thrifty and rewards his people with the excess property in the land, the monarch shall be known as honorable and the people will live easily and in peace.

X

下无直辞，上有隐恶〔170〕

If the courtiers make no just pronouncements and upright suggestions, the monarch will face imminent hidden dangers.

先民而后身〔172〕

In governing a country, the people's affairs should take precedence over the personal affairs of the monarch.

刑罚中于法，废罪顺于民〔174〕

The execution of punishments must meet the requirements of the law. Pardons should be granted following public opinion.

省行者不引其过〔176〕

A man who can examine himself critically can forgive mistakes in others.

Y

以亡为行者不足以存君〔178〕

The man who regards fleeing abroad as a virtue could never defend the monarch.

意莫高于爱民，行莫厚于乐民〔180〕

The noblest thought is to cherish the people, and the best conduct wants only to ensure their happiness.

淫于耳目，不当民务，此圣王之所禁也〔182〕

Concentrating only on his own pleasure and ignoring the administration of the state is in no way how a wise monarch should behave.

愚者多悔，不肖者自贤〔184〕

The men who are foolish are often regretful, and the men who lack virtue often believe themselves to be virtuous and right.

Z

责焉无已，智者有不能给〔186〕

Even the wise cannot do all things impeccably.

政尚相利，故下不以相害为行〔188〕

In governance, advocate mutual benefits, so that people will not do things contrary to their mutual interests.

忠不避死，谏不违罪〔190〕

An honest and faithful courtier is not afraid of death and is not afraid of punishment when he remonstrates against the monarch's mistakes.

忠臣不信，一患也〔192〕

A nation's first hidden danger is the monarch having no trust in his faithful courtiers.

诛暴不避强，替罪不避众〔194〕

To sentence the despots to death and punish the wicked without fear of offending the rich and the influential ...

诛不避贵，赏不遗贱〔196〕

The powerful and influential must be sentenced for violations of the law, just as the common people must not be ignored when rewards are conferred.

从邪害民者有罪，进善举过者有赏〔198〕

The man who poses harm to the people should be known as a criminal. The man who can advise the monarch to redress his faules wisely should be conferred rewards.

左右为社鼠，用事者为猛狗〔200〕

If the attendants to the monarch were like altar rats and the courtiers like savage dogs ...

晏子说

晏子,姓晏名婴,字平仲。春秋齐夷维人。继其父为齐卿,先后事齐灵公、庄公、景公三朝。有人以此说他"事三君,有三心",晏子曰:"三君皆欲其国安,是以婴得顺也。"

晏子以节俭力行重于齐,显名于诸侯,身为齐相,"食不重肉,妾不衣帛",退回君主一切赏赐,心甘情愿"以贫为师"。他提出"廉者,政之本也"的论断,成为后世贤相的榜样。他还主张以礼治国,以礼治民。"国有道,即顺命;无道,即衡命。""君所谓可,而有否焉,臣献其否,以成其可;君所谓否,而有可焉,臣献其可,以去其否。"孔子曰:"晏平仲善与人交,久而敬之。"司马迁为其作传与管仲相提并论,并且说:"假令晏子而在,余虽为之执鞭,所忻慕焉。"

Yan Zi's name was Yan Ying, his courtesy name Pingzhong. He was a native of Yiwei in the State of Qi during the Spring and Autumn Period. He succeeded his father as the prime minister of Qi and served Qi Linggong, Zhuanggong and Jinggong, consecutively. He was thus labeled as "serving three kings with three minds", to which he responded, "All three kings wished for country's stability, so I willingly obeyed them."

Owing to his practice of the principles of thrift and diligence, Yan Zi was held in high regard in Qi and enjoyed enormous prestige among the other states. As the prime minister, Yan Zi never had more than one dish of meat in a meal and his family seldom wore silk clothes. He returned all rewards bestowed upon him by the king and was more than glad to "derive lessons from destitution". He also believed that "honesty and uprightness are the bases of running a state" and hence became a role model for those outstanding prime ministers of subsequent dynasties.

Yan Zi advocated administrating the country and its people with etiquette, stating, "If policies are virtuous and beneficial for the country, then they must be carried out. If they are detrimental to the country, then they must be further considered." "When the monarch thinks something is feasible, the ministers should point out the unfeasible factors so as to fulfill its feasibility; when the monarch finds something is unfeasible, the ministers should point out its feasible aspects in order to remove its unfeasibility." Confucius once noted, "Yan Pingzhong was adept at getting along with others and people revered him." Sima Qian, China's first great historian, wrote a biography of Yan Zi that placed him on par with Guan Zhong, in which he observed, "If Yan Zi were still alive, I would willingly drive his horses for him."

傲大贱小则国危

Scorning large nations and belittling small ones, one's own country will be in peril.

傲大贱小则国危，慢听厚敛则民散。

《晏子春秋·内篇问下》

Scorning large nations and belittling small ones, one's own country will be in peril; handling lawsuits carelessly and imposing taxes heavily, people will become disunited.

【注释】

晏子出使鲁国，鲁昭公问如何使国家安定，使人口众多，晏子对他说了上面的话。

【译文】

傲视大国，轻视小国，国家就危险；处理诉讼轻慢，征收赋税繁重，人民就会离散。

薄于身而厚于民

（**The wise monarchs in ancient times**）led a humble
life while providing adequately for the people.

薄于身而厚于民，约于身而广于世。

《晏子春秋·内篇问上》

(The wise monarchs in ancient times) led a humble life while providing adequately for the people; they practiced frugality while distributing wealth to the public.

【注释】

齐景公问晏子："古代圣明之君，他们的所作所为怎么样？"晏子对他说了上面的话。身：自我，自身。《尔雅·释诂》："朕、余、躬，身也。"注："今人亦自呼为身。"约：节俭。《荀子·荣辱》："约者有筐箧之藏，然而行不敢有舆马。"世：世人。战国屈原《九章·怀沙》："举世皆浊，而我独清。"

【译文】

（古代圣明君主）自己享用微薄，对人民供养丰厚；对自己节俭，钱财广施于世人。

卑而不失尊，曲而不失正者

Those who have a low status but never lose their dignity, who suffer from adversity but still preserve their integrity . . .

卑而不失尊，曲而不失正者，以民为本也。

《晏子春秋·内篇问下》

Those who have a low status but never lose their digni-ty, who suffer from adversity but still preserve their integrity, such men uphold the vision of "people-oriented" govern-ance.

【注释】

晏子认为：世道混乱，君主邪僻，作为臣子地位低不失掉尊严，处境坏不失掉正直，一切"以民为本"。曲：深隐之处，也指偏僻之所。这里指处境不好。以民为本：把人民当成根本。晏子"以民为本"的观点，现在仍然具有进步意义。

【译文】

地位低下但不失掉尊严，处境困难但不失掉正直的人，是把人民当成根本的。

愎谏傲贤者之言，不能威诸侯

The administrative ruler cannot enhance his prestige among other states if he is too stubborn to take advice and despises people of benevolence.

晏子说

惄谏傲贤者之言，不能威诸侯；倍仁义而贪名实者，不能服天下。

《晏子春秋·内篇问上》

The administrative ruler cannot enhance his prestige among other states if he is too stubborn to take advice and despises people of benevolence; nor can he have the world submit to his authority when he betrays justice and humanity or craves fame and wealth.

【注释】

惄谏：固执己见，不听劝谏。惄（bì），固执，任性。《左传·哀公二十七年》："知伯贪而惄，故韩魏反而丧之。" 倍：背弃。《墨子·非儒》："倍本弃事而安怠傲。" 名实：名称和实际，名利。《管子·九守》："名实当则治，不当则乱。"

【译文】

（执政者）固执己见不听劝谏、轻视贤德之人，就不能在诸侯中树立威信；违背仁义、贪图名利的人，就不能让天下人归服。

不劫人以兵甲，不威人以众强

A man who does not coerce the people of other states with military force, or intimidate them with strength in numbers ...

不劫人以兵甲，不威人以众强，故天下皆欲其强。

《晏子春秋·内篇问上》

A man who does not coerce the people of other states with military force, or intimidate them with strength in numbers, such a man is expected by all to be strong and powerful.

【注释】

劫人以兵甲：靠武力胁迫别国人民。劫，威胁，强迫。《左传·庄公八年》："逼贼于门，劫而束之。"兵甲，武力。《出师表》："今南方已定，兵甲已足，当奖率三军，北定中原。"威人以众强：以人多势众欺凌别国人民。威，震慑，欺凌。《战国策·齐策一》："吾三战而三胜，声威天下。"

【译文】

不以武力胁迫别国人民，不靠人多势众欺凌别国人民，所以天下人都希望他势力强大。

不权居以为行，不称位以为忠

A man should not base his own code of conduct on his status; nor decide his necessary degree of loyalty according to his own position.

不权居以为行，不称位以为忠。
不掩贤以隐长，不刻下以谀上。

《晏子春秋·内篇问上》

A man should not base his own code of conduct on his status; nor decide his necessary degree of loyalty according to his own position; he should not discount the strengths of the worthy, nor be severe upon his subordinates while currying favor with his superiors.

【注释】

齐景公问晏子曰："忠臣之行何如?"晏子说了上面的话。权：称量。《孟子·梁惠王上》："权，然后知轻重。"居：处于，位于。《尚书·伊训》："居上克明，为下克忠。"刻下：对下苛刻。

【译文】

不根据自己的地位决定自己行事的准则，不根据自己的地位决定自己的忠诚程度。不压制贤德之人，遮蔽长处，不苛刻对待下级，不阿谀奉承上级。

不掩君过，谏乎前，不华乎外

One should reveal a monarch's mistake by offering advice in his presence but not propagating it.

不掩君过，谏乎前，不华乎外。选贤进能，不私乎内。称身就位，计能定禄。

《晏子春秋·内篇问上》

One should reveal a monarch's mistake by offering advice in his presence but not propagating it. Furthermore, one should select and recommend able people yet not practice favoritism towards one's intimates; hold one's official position with virtue and accept a salary based on one's service.

【注释】

景公问晏子说："忠臣的所作所为是怎样的?"晏子说了上面的话。**华**：通"哗"。此处指宣扬。**称**（chèn）：相当，符合。《荀子·富国》："德必称位，位必称禄，禄必称用。"

【译文】

不掩盖君主的过失，对君主的过失当面劝谏，而不到外面去宣扬。选拔贤德之人，推荐有才能的人，不偏私自己亲近的人。自己的才德和官位相符，根据自己的贡献大小领取俸禄。

不以饮食之辟害民之财

A monarch should not squander people's wealth owing to his own indulgence in food and drink.

不以饮食之辟害民之财，不以宫室之侈劳人之力。

《晏子春秋·内篇问上》

A monarch should not squander people's wealth owing to his own indulgence in food and drink, nor use their labor only to build his own splendid palace.

【注释】

辟（pì）：偏，邪。通"僻"。《论语·先进》："师也辟。"集注："辟，便辟也。"侈（chǐ）：奢侈。《韩非子·解老》："众人之用神也躁，躁则多费，多费之谓侈。"

【译文】

（君主）不因为自己饮食的嗜好而耗费人民的钱财，不因为自己宫室的豪华而役使民力。

不因喜以加赏，不因怒以加罚

A wise monarch must not raise rewards for his personal pleasure, nor increase punishments because of private vendettas.

不因喜以加赏，不因怒以加罚。
不从欲以劳民，不修怒而危国。

《晏子春秋·内篇问上》

A wise monarch must not raise rewards for his personal pleasure, nor increase punishments because of private vendettas; he cannot indulge his personal desires and make the people toil, nor incur the hatred of other nations that could endanger the country.

【注释】

齐景公问晏子说："贤明君主如何治理国家?"晏子说了上面的话。**从欲**：放纵私欲。从（zòng），放纵。通"纵"。《礼记·曲礼上》："欲不可从。" **修怒**：构怨，结怨。

【译文】

（贤明君主治理国家）不因为自己高兴就增加赏赐，不因为自己生气就加重惩罚。不放纵私欲而使百姓劳苦，不与他国结怨而危害国家。

臣有德，益禄；无德，退禄

If a government official is virtuous, increase his salary; if he is not, decrease it.

臣有德，益禄；无德，退禄。

《晏子春秋·内篇杂下》

If a government official is virtuous, increase his salary; if he is not, decrease it.

【注释】

晏子身为齐相，衣食节俭，生活贫困却不肯接受景公给予的食邑，并提出"臣有德，益禄；无德，退禄"的主张。益：增加。退：减少。

【译文】

臣子有德，就增加他的俸禄；无德，就减少他的俸禄。

朝居严则下无言

When the monarch wears a forbidding look at court, his subjects will not dare to speak the truth.

朝居严则下无言，下无言则上无闻矣。下无言，则吾谓之喑；上无闻，则吾谓之聋。聋喑，非害国家而如何也。

《晏子春秋·内篇谏下》

When the monarch wears a forbidding look at court, his subjects will not dare to speak the truth; therefore, he will never be able to hear sound and honest advice. The subjects not speaking the truth, I call "dumb"; the monarch not being able to hear sound and honest advice, I call "deaf". When the monarch is deaf and his subjects dumb, the country is in danger.

【注释】

朝居严：君主在朝廷神情严厉。朝，朝廷，帝王上朝议事之处。《孟子·梁惠王上》："使天下仕者皆欲立于王之朝。"严，严厉，严格。《孙子·计篇》："将者，智、信、仁、勇、严也。"《史记·太史公自序》："法家严而少恩。"喑（yīn）：哑。

【译文】

君主在朝廷神情严厉，臣子就不敢讲真话；臣子不讲真话，那么君主就听不到正确意见。臣子不讲真话，我把这叫做"哑"；君主听不到正确意见，我把这叫做"聋"。上聋下哑，不是对国家有害又是什么！

春省耕而补不足者谓之游

Examining crop cultivations in spring and offering help to those in need, this inspection tour of the past monarchs is called "yóu".

春省耕而补不足者谓之游，秋省实而助不给者谓之豫。

《晏子春秋·内篇问下》

Examining crop cultivations in spring and offering help to those in need, this inspection tour of the past monarchs is called "yóu"; examining harvests in autumn and granting subsidies to those whose crops failed, this inspection tour is called "yù".

【注释】

晏子指出，古代君主春天出游是为了考察百姓耕种情况从而对耕种困难者给以帮助，秋天出游是为了考察收获情况从而对歉收者给以补助。批评齐景公出游只是纵情山水，狩猎享乐。省（xǐng）：考察。《易·观》："先王以省方观民设教。"（秋）豫：指帝王秋天出巡。

【译文】

古代君主春天考察耕种情况，对耕种困难者给以帮助，这叫做游；秋天检查收获情况，对歉收者给以补助，这叫做豫。

从高历时而不反谓之流，从下而不反谓之连

Indulging in visits to mountain scenery and not thinking of returning is called "liú"; indulging in visits to water scenery and not thinking of returning is called "lián".

从高历时而不反谓之流，从下而不反谓之连，从兽而不归谓之荒，从乐而不归谓之亡。古者圣王无流连之游、荒亡之行。

《晏子春秋·内篇问下》

Indulging in visits to mountain scenery and not thinking of returning is called "liú"; indulging in visits to water scenery and not thinking of returning is called "lián"; indulging in hunting activities and not thinking of returning is called "huāng"; and indulging in merry-making and not thinking of returning is called "wáng". None of the ancient wise monarchs ever did such things when going on an outing.

【注释】

从高历时而不反谓之流：纵情游山超过了时间不回去叫做流。从（zòng），纵情。同"纵"。反，同"返"。**流连**：乐而忘返。《孟子·梁惠王下》："流连荒亡，为诸侯忧。从流下而忘反谓之流，从流上而忘反谓之连，……先王无流连之乐。"

【译文】

纵情游山赏景不知归叫做流，纵情游水不知归叫做连，纵情狩猎不知归叫做荒，纵情作乐不知归叫做亡。古代圣贤君主出游没有这些流连荒亡的行为。

寸之管，无当，天下不能足之以粟

A bottomless bamboo pipe, short as one *cun*, can never be filled though all the grain in the world be put inside it.

寸之管，无当，天下不能足之以粟。

《晏子春秋·内篇谏下》

A bottomless bamboo pipe, short as one *cun*, can never be filled though all the grain in the world be put inside it.

【注释】

齐景公赋敛沉重，狱讼繁多，监狱里关满了人，到处是怨恨的情绪。晏子指出，治理国家应该居上位处事公正，居下位依礼行事，限制大臣们的贪欲。寸之管，无当：一寸长的竹管，如果没有底，就永远装不满。以此比喻君主贪欲无度。晏子说："今齐国丈夫耕，女子织，夜以接日，不足以奉上，而君侧皆雕文刻镂之观，此无当之管也，而君终不知。"当（dàng），底，器物的底部。《韩非子·外储说右上》："堂谿公谓昭侯曰：'今有千金之玉卮而无当，可以盛水乎？'"卮（zhī），古代盛酒的器皿。

【译文】

一寸长的竹管，如果没有底，天下的粮食也不能把它装满。

德薄而禄厚，智惛而家富，是彰
污而逆教也

It is an act of condoning corruption which goes a-
gainst the sages' teachings to have someone lacking in
virtue enjoy a high salary or someone injudicious live in
plenty.

德薄而禄厚，智惛而家富，是彰污而逆教也。

《晏子春秋·内篇杂下》

It is an act of condoning corruption which goes against the sages' teachings to have someone lacking in virtue enjoy a high salary or someone injudicious live in plenty.

【注释】

晏子年老，请求归还食邑，景公不许，晏子说了上面的话。**惛**（hūn）：神智不清。《庄子·知北游》："惛然若亡而存。"《孟子·梁惠王上》："吾惛，不能进于是矣。" **逆教**：违背圣贤的教诲。

【译文】

德行浅薄却俸禄丰厚，神志昏聩却家中富足，这是表彰贪腐，是违背圣贤教诲的。

德不足以怀人，政不足以惠民

If the ruler fails to get his people to cherish his morals and to have his politics benefit his people . . .

德不足以怀人，政不足以惠民。赏不足以劝善，刑不足以防非。亡国之行也。

《晏子春秋·内篇问上》

It will be the downfall of the country if the ruler fails to get his people to cherish his morals and to have his politics benefit his people; his rewards fail to encourage people to do good and his punishments fail to prevent them from committing bad deeds.

【注释】

这是晏子对古代无道君主的批评，也是对齐景公的告诫。**怀**：想念。《诗经·周南·卷耳》："嗟我怀人，寘（zhì）彼周行。"**惠**：恩惠。《国语·晋语》："未报楚惠而抗宋，我曲楚直。"**劝**：勉励。《论语·为政》："举善而教不能则劝。"**非**：过失。《孟子·告子上》："是非之心，人皆有之。"

【译文】

道德不足以让人民怀念，政治不足以让人民获得好处。赏赐起不到鼓励人做好事的作用，刑罚起不到防止人干坏事的作用。这些是使国家灭亡的行为啊。

德厚而受禄，德薄则辞禄

When one has morals and virtuous conduct, they should receive a salary; when one lacks morals and virtuous conduct, they should return it.

德厚而受禄，德薄则辞禄。德厚受禄，所以明上矣；德薄辞禄，可以洁下矣。

《晏子春秋·内篇杂下》

When one has morals and virtuous conduct, they should receive a salary; when one lacks morals and virtuous conduct, they should return it. Receiving a salary is to demonstrate the monarch's brilliance, returning it is to have the subjects preserve their incorruptibility.

【注释】

晏子为齐相，年老，请求归还食邑。景公说齐国从开国至今，没有哪位大夫年老时归还食邑的。晏子说，古代侍奉君主的人，衡量自己的德行然后接受俸禄。德行厚就接受俸禄，德行薄就归还俸禄。德行厚接受俸禄是为了彰显君主的英明，德行薄归还俸禄，是为了让臣子保持廉洁。我年已老，德行微薄，却接受厚禄，这对上对下都没有好处。

【译文】

德行深厚就接受俸禄，德行浅薄就归还俸禄。德行深厚而接受俸禄是为了彰显君主的英明，德行浅薄而归还俸禄是为了让臣子保持廉洁。

德行教诲加于诸侯，慈爱利泽加于百姓

Influencing other states by virtue and morality, treating the people with affection and kindness . . .

德行教诲加于诸侯，慈爱利泽加于百姓，故海内归之若流水。

《晏子春秋·内篇问上》

Influencing other states by virtue and morality, treating the people with affection and kindness, such a leader will have all people flocking to him just like flowing water joining the sea.

【注释】

德行：道德，品行。《易·节》："君子以制数度，议德行。"疏："德行谓人才堪任之优劣。"**慈爱**：仁慈，爱人。《国语·楚语上》："明慈爱以道之仁，明昭利以道之文。"**利**：利益，功用。《商君书·算地》："利出于地，则民尽力。"**泽**：恩德，恩泽。《尚书·毕命》："道洽政治，泽润生民。"**海内**：中国古人认为中国四周皆环海，故称国境以内为海内，犹言天下。

【译文】

以道德品行教诲感化诸侯，以仁慈爱人恩惠施于百姓，所以天下人民会像江水归附大海一样归附于他。

地不同生，人不同能

Like lands are of different properties, people are of different abilities.

地不同生，而任之以一种，责其俱生，不可得；人不同能，而任之以一事，不可责遍成。

《晏子春秋·内篇问上》

It is impossible to grow the same crop on lands of different properties; likewise, one can never appoint people of different abilities with the same task and expect all of them to be qualified for it.

【注释】

齐景公问晏子曰："古代执政者如何任用人才？"晏子说了上面的话，意为量材选用，不可求全责备。生：本性，天性。同"性"。《尚书·君陈》："惟民生厚，因物有迁。"传："言人自然之性敦厚，因所见所习之物有变迁之道。"《商君书·开塞》："民之生，不知则学。"责：要求。《荀子·宥坐》："不教而责成功，虐也。"

【译文】

土地的性质不一样，却种植同一种作物，要求不同性质的土地都能生长这种作物，是不可能的；人的才能不一样，却委任一样的工作，不能要求他们都能胜任这一工作。

夫社，束木而涂之，鼠因往托焉

Rats find a safe place to live in the altar which is built by binding the wood and then applying mud on it.

夫社，束木而涂之，鼠因往托焉。熏之则恐烧其木，灌之则恐败其涂。此鼠所以不可得杀者，以社故也。

《晏子春秋·内篇问上》

Rats find a safe place to live in the altar which is built by binding the wood and then applying mud on it. Man cannot smoke out the rats for fear of burning the wood, nor can drown them with water lest they flood the mud walls. It is the altar itself that provides the shelter for the rats, and that is the reason why they cannot be exterminated.

【注释】

齐景公问晏子治理国家的祸害是什么，晏子回答说是寄居在社坛的老鼠：既不能用水浇，又不能用烟熏。晏子以"社鼠"比喻景公身边的侍从。故曰："夫国亦有焉，人主左右是也。" **束木而涂之：** 捆扎木头并涂上泥。

【译文】

社坛是捆扎木头并涂上泥做成的，老鼠住在里边。用烟熏怕烧掉木头，用水灌怕泡塌泥墙。这老鼠之所以不能被除掉，是因为有社坛的保护。

富而不骄者，未尝闻之

To lead an abundant life yet not domineering, such a man has never been heard of.

富而不骄者，未尝闻之；贫而不恨者，婴是也。所以贫而不恨者，以若为师也。

《晏子春秋·内篇杂下》

To lead an abundant life yet not domineering, such a man has never been heard of; to live a poor life yet without any regret, I am such a man for I regard poverty as my teacher.

【注释】

晏子以廉洁节俭有名于世，身居相位，一直过着清贫的生活。他多次拒绝齐景公的赏赐，反对为其扩建住宅，甚至坚持交出自己的俸禄、食邑和车马。他之所以能做到"贫而不恨"，甚至"以贫为师"，是因为他认为廉洁节俭"可以洁下"，可以影响下属，可以防止世风的侈靡，其用心可谓良苦。

【译文】

家中富足而不骄横的人，没有听说过；贫穷但无遗憾的人，我就是这样的人。我之所以贫穷而无遗憾，是因为我是以贫为师的人。

古之王者，德厚足以安世

Those who proclaimed themselves kings in ancient times all had virtues that guaranteed social stability.

古之王者，德厚足以安世，行广足以容众。诸侯戴之，以为君长；百姓归之，以为父母。

《晏子春秋·内篇谏上》

Those who proclaimed themselves kings in ancient times all had virtues that guaranteed social stability, and broad minds that tolerates their people. Leaders of other states supported them as superiors, and their people regarded them as parental figures.

【注释】

齐景公相信楚国巫者的话，举行斋戒活动，晏子对此给予批评，讲了上面的话。**德**：道德。《易·乾·文言》："君子进德修业。" **行**（旧读 xìng）：行为。《论语·公冶长》："今吾于人也，听其言而观其行。" **容**：容纳，宽容。《庄子·庚桑楚》："不能容人者无亲。"《尚书·君陈》："有容，德乃大。" 疏："有所宽容，其德乃能大。"

【译文】

古代称王的人，道德淳厚足以使社会安定；胸怀广阔足以包容众人。诸侯爱戴他，把他尊为君长；百姓归附他，把他当成父母。

古之贤君，饱而知人之饥

The wise monarchs in ancient times knew there were common people who were hungry while they themselves were full.

古之贤君，饱而知人之饥，温而知人之寒，逸而知人之劳。

《晏子春秋·内篇谏上》

The wise monarchs in ancient times knew there were common people who were hungry while they themselves were full, people who were cold while they themselves dressed in warm clothes, and people who worked strenuously while they themselves were living in ease.

【注释】

齐景公身穿狐裘，奇怪大雪天却不寒冷，晏子批评他不知道百姓饥寒疾苦，促其施行善政。孔子听说了这件事后说："晏子能明其所欲，景公能行其所善也。"

【译文】

古代贤明的君主，自己吃饱却知道有人在挨饿，自己穿暖却知道有人在受冻，自己安逸却知道有人劳累不堪。

古者先君之干福也，政必合乎民

In ancient times, the monarch could pray for blessings only when his policies followed the people's hearts.

古者先君之干福也，政必合乎民，行必顺乎神。

《晏子春秋·内篇问上》

In ancient times, the emperor could pray for blessings only when his policies followed the people's hearts, and his behavior was righteous.

【注释】

齐景公想通过祭祀上帝和祖庙而求福。晏子对他说古代君主政令符合民心，行为顺应神意，祭祀只是悔过而不敢求福。**干福**：求福。干，求取。《荀子·议兵》："兼是数国者，干赏蹈利之兵也。"

【译文】

古代君主求福，施政必定符合民心，行为必定顺应天意。

古之饮酒也，足以通气合好而
已矣

    The function of drinking in ancient times was only to invigorate blood circulation and entertain guests.

古之饮酒也，足以通气合好而已
矣。故男不群乐以妨事，女不群乐以
妨功。

《晏子春秋·内篇谏上》

The function of drinking in ancient times was only to invigorate blood circulation and entertain guests. Thus, drinking could not hinder either men's work or women's needlework.

【注释】

齐景公喝醉酒三天不理朝政，晏子劝谏说，喝酒不过是为了疏通气脉，娱乐宾客而已，应该有所节制，不能因为饮酒妨害本职工作。**合好**：关系融洽。《国语·周语》："酬币宴货，以示容合好。"指和客人关系融洽。**事**：本业，正事。**功**：女红。

【译文】

古时候的人喝酒，不过是用来疏通气脉或者为了宴请宾客而已。所以男子不会聚饮而影响本职工作，妇女不会聚饮而妨害女红。

观之以其游，说之以其行

We should judge a man by observing his friends and his behaviors.

观之以其游，说之以其行。君无以靡曼辩辞定其行，无以毁誉非议定其身。

《晏子春秋·内篇问上》

We should judge a man by observing his friends and his behaviors, and should place no credence on boastful words of his own or the comments of others.

【注释】

齐景公问晏子求贤的方法，晏子说了上面的话。**游**：交游，交结的朋友。《礼记·典礼上》："交游称其信也。"**说**：评说，评价。**靡曼**：华丽。《墨子·辞过》："必厚作敛于百姓，暴夺民衣食之财，以为锦绣文采靡曼之衣……单财劳力，毕归之于无用。"此处指言辞华丽。

【译文】

通过他交往的那些人来观察他，通过他的所作所为来评价他。不根据他华丽的言辞和善辩的口才来判定他的行为，也不根据别人对他的非议诋毁或赞誉来判定他的为人。

棺椁衣衾，不以害生养

The cost of a coffin and funeral clothes should not be too high, in case it becomes a burden on the living.

棺椁衣衾，不以害生养，哭泣处哀，不以害生道。

《晏子春秋·内篇谏下》

The cost of a coffin and funeral clothes should not be too high, in case it becomes a burden on the living, while the sorrow and mourning of the living should not influence their long term health.

【注释】

棺椁：内棺叫棺，外棺叫椁。古代葬埋有棺有椁，套在棺外面的叫椁。衾（qīn）：覆盖尸体的单被。《孝经·丧亲》："为之棺椁衣衾而举之。"疏："衾，谓单被，覆尸荐尸所用。"《韩非子·内储说上》："齐国好厚葬，布帛尽于衣衾，材木尽于棺椁。"

【译文】

（人死后）棺椁衣被不过分耗费，不让这些耗费损害活人的需求；哭泣悲哀应该有所节制，不能因此损害养生之道。

贵不凌贱，富不傲贫

The nobles should not insult the commoners, the rich should not be arrogant in front of the poor.

贵不凌贱，富不傲贫；功不遗
罢，佞不吐愚；举事不私，听狱
不阿。

《晏子春秋·内篇问上》

The nobles should not insult the commoners, the rich should not be arrogant in front of the poor, the meritorious should not disregard the futile, the clever should not despise the fool, and the officers should be impartial when performing their duties and settling lawsuits.

【注释】

齐景公想让晏子辅佐自己好像管子辅佐先君桓公一样成就霸业。晏子对景公详细陈说桓公时期的种种善政。**功不遗罢，佞不吐愚**：有功绩的人不遗弃无功之人，聪明人不鄙弃愚笨之人。罢（pí），疲困，软弱。通"疲"。《韩非子·说林上》："魏攻中山而弗能取，则魏必罢，罢则魏轻。"佞（nìng），才。《左传·成公十三年》："寡人不佞。"自谦无能称不佞。吐，抛弃。

【译文】

尊贵者不欺侮卑贱者，富裕的人不轻视贫穷者；有功之人不遗弃劳而无功者，聪明的人不鄙弃愚拙之人；处事不徇私情，断案公正无私。

贵戚不荐善，逼迩不引过

If important ministers do not give good counsel and officials close to the monarch do not point out his mistakes . . .

贵戚不荐善，逼迩不引过，反圣王之德，而循灭君之行。

《晏子春秋·内篇谏上》

If important ministers do not give good counsel and officials close to the monarch do not point out his mistakes, it will be detrimental to the virtues of a wise monarch and lead to the country's fall.

【注释】

这是晏子谏齐庄公的话。**贵戚**：同姓的显贵大臣。《孟子·万章下》："有贵戚之卿，有异姓之卿。"**荐善**：进善言。荐，进。《易·豫》："殷荐之上帝，以配祖考。"**逼迩**：指近臣。逼，迫近。**不引过**：见过错不劝谏。引，称引。**循**：沿着，顺着。**灭君**：亡国之君。灭，亡。

【译文】

（君主身边）显贵的大臣不进善言，亲近的大臣见过错不劝谏，违反圣贤君主的道德，步亡国之君的后尘。

国有道，即顺命

If policies are virtuous and beneficial for the country, then they must be carried out.

国有道，即顺命；无道，即衡命。

《史记·管晏列传》

If policies are virtuous and beneficial for the country, then they must be carried out. If they are detrimental to the country, then they must be further considered and only carried out with great discretion.

【注释】

晏子事齐灵公、庄公、景公三朝，以节俭力行重于齐，身为齐相，食不重肉，妾不衣帛。其在朝，君语及之，即危言；语不及之，即危行。国有道，即顺命；无道，即衡命。以此三世显名于诸侯。**衡命**：衡，称也。谓国无道则制称量之，可行即行。

【译文】

国家政策法令符合道义，就顺从君主的命令；不合道义，衡量得失，斟酌命令的情况，可行即行。

国有三不祥

A country has three evil omens.

国有三不祥：夫有贤而不知，一不祥；知而不用，二不祥；用而不任，三不祥也。

《晏子春秋·内篇谏下》

A country has three evil omens. The first is when administrative rulers do not know who are the virtuous and talented people in their countries. The second is when administrative rulers know there are virtuous and talented people, but do not employ them. The third is when administrative rulers employ the virtuous and talented, but they do not entrust them with important positions.

【注释】

齐景公上山见虎，下泽见蛇以为不祥。晏子指出，山上本来就有老虎的家，沼泽本来就有蛇的洞穴，所以见虎见蛇不能算不祥，对国家来说真正不祥的事有三件。任：任用。《尚书·大禹谟》："任贤勿贰。"

【译文】

国家有三件不吉祥的事：有贤德之人而不知道，这是一不吉祥；知道了而不能使用，这是二不吉祥；使用却不能委以重任，这是三不吉祥。

合升斗之微，以满仓廪

A full granary begins with a single *sheng*.

合升斗之微，以满仓廪；合疏缕之纬，以成帷幕。

《晏子春秋·内篇谏下》

A full granary begins with a single *sheng*; cloth begins with a single thread.

【注释】

升斗之微：一升一斗量微不足道。升斗，升为容量的基本单位，斗为计量常用单位，古籍中多升斗连用，比喻微薄，少量。《汉书·梅福传》："言：可采取者，秩以升斗之禄，赐以一束之帛。" 疏：稀。《老子》第73章："天网恢恢，疏而不失。" 纬：织物上的横线。帷幕：帐幕。帷，帐。通"帷"。《史记·文帝纪》："所幸慎夫人，令衣不得曳地，帷帐不得文绣，以示敦朴。"

【译文】

聚合一升一斗就能装满粮仓，聚合织物上稀疏的横线就能织成帐幕。

见善必通，不私其利

Officials should implement good policies immediately without intending to seek personal gain.

见善必通，不私其利。荐善而不有其名。称身居位，不为苟进。称事授禄，不为苟得。

《晏子春秋·内篇问下》

Officials should implement good policies immediately without intending to seek personal gain; recommend the virtuous and capable without planning to build their own reputations; undertake posts according to their own abilities not because they crave high positions; accept salaries that are in accord with their own contributions not because they seek personal wealth.

【注释】

景公问为臣之道，晏子列举九条做臣子应遵守的准则，把实行善政、举荐贤人、不苟且求官、不苟且求财、不谋私利放在重要位置。通：畅通，实行。《易·系辞上》："一阖一辟谓之变，往来不穷谓之通。"

【译文】

看到好的政令一定去实行，不从中谋取私利。推举贤德的人不是贪图荐贤的好名声。衡量自己的才能担任适当的职位，不苟且求官。衡量自己的贡献接受适当的俸禄，不苟且贪财。

见贤不留，使能不怠

The monarch should employ the virtuous and capable as soon as they are found, and after employing them should never neglect them.

见贤不留，使能不怠。

《晏子春秋·内篇问下》

The monarch should employ the virtuous and capable as soon as they are found, and after employing them should never neglect them.

【注释】

齐景公问晏子说："从前我们的先君桓公也好饮酒作乐，爱好女色，为什么还能称霸诸侯呢？"晏子说："先君桓公虽有这些过失，但其能以政令改变旧俗，能礼贤下士，任贤使能。因此，处理内政，人民亲附他，出兵征讨，诸侯畏惧他，所以成就了王霸大业。"**留**：存留。《墨子·非儒下》："于是厚其礼，留其封，敬见而不问其道。"**怠**：怠慢。

【译文】

遇到贤德之人就任用，没有遗漏；任用有才能的人，不敢怠慢他们。

见贤而进之，不同君所欲

**Virtuous and capable people must be promoted,
even if the monarch disagrees with their advancement.**

见贤而进之，不同君所欲；见不善则废之，不辟君所爱。行己而无私，直言而无讳。

《晏子春秋·外篇》

Virtuous and capable people must be promoted, even if the monarch disagrees with their advancement. Evildoers must be removed, even if the monarch indulges them. Everything should be done impartially and the monarch should be advised with straightforward honesty.

【注释】

晏子为齐相，遇见贤德的人就提拔他，不求和君主的想法相同；遇到品德不好的人就罢免他，不回避他是君主所宠爱的人。所作所为秉公无私，对君主直言劝谏不加避讳。有人向齐景公进谗言，任免官员不和君主保持一致是专断；对君主直言劝谏，不加避讳是傲慢。专断和傲慢的人怎么能算忠臣呢！景公果然听信谗言，对晏子表现出不满，晏子遂上书辞职而不悔。

【译文】

（晏子）看到贤德的人就提拔他，不求和君主的想法相同；看到品德不好的人就罢免他，不回避君主所宠爱的人。所作所为秉公无私，对君主直言劝谏无所避讳。

禁之以制，而身不先行，民不
能止

If the administration wishes to impose bans, they
themselves must follow them first. Otherwise, it will be
impossible to convince the common men to obey them.

禁之以制，而身不先行，民不能止。

《晏子春秋·内篇杂下》

If the administration wishes to impose bans, they themselves must follow them first. Otherwise, it will be impossible to convince the common men to obey them.

【注释】

晏子认为，以制度禁止人们的某些行为，居上位者必先作出表率；要改变民心，身教重于言教。

【译文】

（居上位的人）用制度禁止（某项活动），而自身不能先作出表率，就无法制止百姓。

尽智导民而不伐焉

The wise monarchs in ancient times tried their best to guide their people to goodness, and did not boast of their achievements.

尽智导民而不伐焉，劳力岁事而不责焉。

《晏子春秋·内篇问上》

The wise monarchs in ancient times tried their best to guide their people to goodness, and did not boast of their achievements. They encouraged people to be devoted to developing agriculture, but did not make excessive demands of their people.

【注释】

齐景公问晏子曰："古之圣君，其行如何?"晏子对曰："薄于身而厚于民，约于身而广于世；其处上也，足以明政行教，不以威天下；其取财也，权有无，均贫富，不以养嗜欲；诛不避贵，赏不遗贱；不淫于乐，不遁于哀；尽智导民而不伐焉，劳力岁事而不责焉。"**尽智导民**：用尽才智引导人民向善。**伐**：自夸其功劳和才能叫伐。《论语·雍也》："孟之反不伐。" **岁事**：指农事。《尚书大传·略说》："岁事既毕，余子皆入学。"

【译文】

（古代圣明君主）用尽才智引导人民向善，但不自夸其功劳；鼓励人民勤劳于农事，但不苛求人民。

进不失廉，退不失行

Officers should be free of corruption when holding their position and keep their upright characters after withdrawal from their position.

进不失廉，退不失行。

《晏子春秋·内篇问上》

Officers should be free of corruption when holding their position and keep their upright characters after withdrawal from their position.

【注释】

晏子曰："察士不比周而进，不为苟而求。言无阴阳，行无内外。顺则进，否则退，不与上行邪。是以进不失廉，退不失行也。"**进不失廉**：当官时不丧失自己的廉洁。进，就其所处地位向前、向上都称为进。**退**：与"进"相对。此处进退作仕进和隐退解。

【译文】

做官不丧失自己的廉洁，隐退不丧失自己的品行。

俭于藉敛，节于货财

Levying taxes should be moderate, the use of property should be frugal.

俭于藉敛，节于货财。作工不历时，使民不尽力。

《晏子春秋·内篇问上》

Levying taxes should be moderate, the use of property should be frugal. Using manpower for other purposes should not delay the farming season. The labor of the people should not be excessive.

【注释】

齐景公问晏子："怎样做才能让人民亲附?"晏子说："征收赋税要节制，使用财物要节俭。兴建土木工程不误农时，役使百姓不使尽民力。各种官吏设置精干恰当，减少关市税收，不垄断山林池泽。治理人民而不使他们反感，不要让人民挨饿受冻。这样的话，人民就会亲附您。"**历时**：误农时。历，过。**尽力**：竭尽材力。《管子·形势》："人主之所以使下尽力而亲上者，必为天下致利害也。"

【译文】

征收赋税要节制，使用财物要节俭。征发民工不误农时，役使百姓不竭尽其力。

节欲则民富，中听则民安

If the administrative rulers moderate their desires,
the people will be rich. If lawsuits are carried out fairly,
the people will live in harmony.

节欲则民富，中听则民安。

《晏子春秋·内篇问下》

If the administrative rulers moderate their desires, the people will be rich. If lawsuits are carried out fairly, the people will live in harmony.

【注释】

景公问富民安众之策，晏子说："君主节制私欲，人民就会富裕；处理诉讼公正，人民就会安定。"**中听**：处理诉讼恰当。中，合适，恰当。听，断决，治理。《周礼·秋官·小司寇》："以五声听狱讼，求民情：一曰辞听，二曰色听，三曰气听，四曰耳听，五曰目听。"

【译文】

（执政者）节制私欲，人民就会富裕；处理诉讼公正，人民（社会）就会安定。

近臣默，远臣喑，众口铄金

When the ministers in the court keep their mouths shut and the ministers out of court pretend to be dumb, the criticism from the people could melt even metal.

晏子说

近臣默，远臣喑，众口铄金。

《晏子春秋·内篇谏上》

When the ministers in the court keep their mouths shut and the ministers out of court pretend to be dumb, the criticism from the people could melt even metal.

【注释】

齐景公患病经年不愈，要杀死为之祈祷的两个官吏。晏子说，您疏远辅佐的人，忠臣被阻隔，无人说劝谏的话，近臣默不作声，远臣装聋作哑，众人的话可以熔化金属，现在全国的人批评您的话太多了，靠两个祈祷的官吏会有作用吗？**近臣默：**身边的臣子默不作声。近臣，君主左右亲近之臣。默，不语。《易·系辞上》："君子之道，或出或处，或默或语。" **远臣喑：**外臣哑口无言。远臣，外臣。喑（yīn），缄默不言。《墨子·亲士》："臣下重其爵位而不言，近臣则喑。" **众口铄金：**众人异口同声的言论，足以熔化金属。比喻舆论力量大。铄（shuò），熔化。《国语·周语下》："故谚曰：'众心成城，众口铄金。'"

【译文】

朝臣默不作声，外臣哑口无言，人民异口同声的言论足以熔化金属。

橘生淮南则为橘，生于淮北则为枳

The orange growing in the south was sweet, but that in the north was sour.

橘生淮南则为橘，生于淮北则为枳，叶徒相似，其实味不同。所以然者何？水土异也。今民生长于齐不盗，入楚则盗，得无楚之水土使民善盗耶？

《晏子春秋·内篇杂下》

The orange growing in the south was sweet, but that in the north was sour. They had similar leaves, but different tastes. Why? The reason was that the environments were different. Now, that man did not steal when he lived in the State of Qi, but he became a thief after entering the State of Chu. Did the environment of the State of Chu make that man become a thief more easily?

【注释】

晏子出使楚国，楚王和近侍为羞辱晏子，在朝廷上演出一场诬陷齐人为盗的闹剧，晏子机智地以橘树过淮北为枳为喻，反过来羞辱了楚国君臣，维护了自己和齐国的尊严。枳（zhǐ）：果树名，实酸苦，可入药。橘和枳是两种不同的果树，并非橘过淮北为枳，这是晏子机智的辩辞。

【译文】

橘树生长在淮水以南叫橘树，生长在淮水以北就变成了枳树，这两种树叶形相似，果实味道大不一样。为什么会这样呢？这是因为水土不相同的缘故。现在这个人在齐国并不偷盗，进入楚国就偷盗，该不会是楚国的水土使人变得善于偷盗的吧？

举贤以临国，官能以敕民，则其
道也

The best way to administer a country is to employ
the virtuous and capable.

举贤以临国，官能以敕民，则其道也。举贤官能，则民兴善矣。

《晏子春秋·内篇问上》

The best way to administer a country is to employ the virtuous and capable. Employing the virtuous and capable will guide the people to goodness and prosperity.

【注释】

齐景公问晏子曰："莅国治民，善为国家者何如？"晏子说了上面的话。临国：治理国家。临，统管，治理。《国语·晋语》："苟从是行也，临长晋国者，非汝其谁？"官能：职能。《礼记·礼器》："人官有能也。"疏："人居其官，各有所能，若司徒奉牛，司马奉羊，及庖人治庖，祝治尊俎是也。"此处意为授官给有才能的人。敕（chì）：整饬，治理。

【译文】

提拔贤德的人治理国家，选用有才能的人管理百姓，这就是古代圣贤君主治理国家的办法。提拔贤德的人，任用有才能的人，人民就会向善。

举之以语，考之以事

A man should be recommended according to his words, and assessed according to his deeds.

举之以语，考之以事。能谕则尚
而亲之，近而勿辱。以取人，则得贤
之道也。

《晏子春秋·内篇问上》

A man should be recommended according to his words,
and assessed according to his deeds. If he knows how to administer a country, then he should be promoted and drawn
closer to the ruler, while ensuring that his closeness is main-
tained without impropriety. This is the way to obtain the loyalty of the virtuous and capable.

【注释】

景公问得贤之道，晏子对此举之以语，考之以事。意即根据他说的话推举他，
根据他的行事考察他，把考察言语与行事结合起来，就能得到贤德之人。谕（yù）：
知道，理解。《荀子·儒效》："其言多当矣，而未谕也。"

【译文】

根据他的言语举荐他，根据他的行事考察他。证明
他能够通晓治国之道，就选拔而亲近他，虽亲近而不废
上下间的礼仪。这是得到贤德之人的正确方法。

君国者不乐民之哀

The ruler of a country should not base his happiness on the pain of his people.

君国者不乐民之哀。

《晏子春秋·内篇谏下》

The ruler of a country should not base his happiness on the pain of his people.

【注释】

齐景公征发夫役修建大台，刚完工又欲铸造编钟。晏子指出，君主欲望无穷，必然加重赋税，给百姓造成痛苦。并说："敛民之哀而以为乐，不祥，非所以君国者。"**君国者：**当国家君主的人。君，统治，主宰。《荀子·王霸》："合天下而君之。"

【译文】

作为国君，不把自己的快乐建立在百姓的痛苦之上。

君屈民财者不得其利

The monarch who exhausts the property of the nation cannot achieve personal gain.

君屈民财者不得其利，穷民力者不得其乐。

《晏子春秋·内篇谏下》

The monarch who exhausts the property of the nation and the labor of people cannot and the labor of people achieve personal gain or find happiness for himself.

【注释】

齐景公连年征发徭役，使老百姓困苦不堪。晏子进谏并以楚灵王兴役不止最终身死乾溪的教训劝景公停止劳民工程。屈（jué）：竭尽，穷尽。《庄子·天运》："目知穷乎所欲见，力屈乎所欲逐。"《荀子·王制》："使国家足用，而财物不屈。"

【译文】

君主耗尽民财自己难得其利；用尽民力自己难得快乐。

君人者与其请于人，不如请于己也

If the monarchs want their descendants to succeed them to the throne, it is better to ask help from themselves than from others.

君人者与其请于人，不如请于己也。

《晏子春秋·内篇谏下》

If the monarchs want their descendants to succeed them to the throne, it is better to ask help from themselves than from others.

【注释】

齐景公想把君位传给子孙，但却把聚敛的财物存放坏也不肯发放给饥民，还对百姓横征暴敛。晏子说：将来掌握齐国政权的，一定是能让百姓得利的人。因此，想传君位给子孙，与其求助于人，不如求自己。**请：**请求，要求。《左传·隐公元年》："亟请于武公，公弗许。"

【译文】

当君主的如果想把君位传给子孙，与其求助别人，不如反躬自求。

君正臣从谓之顺

The minister who obeys the right order of the monarch's is a faithful minister.

君正臣从谓之顺，君僻臣从谓之逆。

《晏子春秋·内篇谏下》

The minister who obeys the right order of the monarch's is a faithful minister, but if he obeys the wrong order of the monarch's, he is a treacherous one.

【注释】

齐景公宠妾死后，非常伤心，守着她的尸体不让葬埋，希望她能死而复生。晏子假称能够让她起死回生，让景公离开后便命人将尸体葬埋。景公知道后责备晏子欺骗他，晏子说了上面的话。顺：顺从，顺应。与"逆"相对。《易·革》："小人革面，顺以从君也。"僻：邪僻。《论语·先进》："师也僻。"逆：不顺。《尚书·太甲下》："有言逆于汝心，必求诸道。"

【译文】

君主意见正确臣子服从叫做顺从，君主邪僻臣子服从叫做背逆。

君子不怀暴君之禄

Gentlemen do not covet rewards offered by tyrants.

君子不怀暴君之禄，不处乱国之位。

《晏子春秋·内篇问下》

Gentlemen do not covet rewards offered by tyrants, and do not take up positions of power in turbulent countries.

【注释】

晏子奉命出使吴国，吴王问：君子如何决定在一个国家任职或离开？晏子回答说：应该根据这个国家的治乱情况而定。"婴闻之，亲疏得处其伦，大臣得尽其忠，民无怨治，国无虐刑，则可处矣。""亲疏不得居其伦，大臣不得尽其忠，民多怨治，国有虐刑，则可去矣。"**暴君：**残暴君主。暴，凶恶。《易·系辞上》："上慢下暴，盗思伐之矣。"**乱国：**混乱不安定的国家。《管子·治国》："故治国常富，而乱国常贫。"

【译文】

君子不贪恋残暴君主的俸禄，不在混乱不安定的国家任职。

君子独立不惭于影

A gentleman does not feel shame when he stands alone in front of his shadow.

君子独立不惭于影，独寝不惭于魂。

《晏子春秋·外篇》

A gentleman does not feel shame when he stands alone in front of his shadow, just as when he sleeps alone he does not feel shame in his soul.

【注释】

孔子到齐国去，谒见齐景公后却不肯会见晏子。子贡说："谒见君主却不见执政的人，可以吗？"孔子说："我听说晏子侍奉三位齐君而且都能顺从他们，我怀疑晏子的为人。"晏子听到这话后说了上面的话。孔子听后惭愧地说："丘闻过人以为友，不及人以为师。今丘失言于夫子，夫子讥之，是吾师也。"因让弟子去道歉，然后会见晏子。这反映了晏子的磊落和孔子的"过则勿惮改"精神，彰显两位贤圣之美。

【译文】

君子独自站立无愧于身影，独自睡卧无愧于梦魂。

君子居必择居，游必就士

If a gentleman wishes to find a living place, he must make a good choice in his neighbors; when he embarks upon a journey, he must find someone virtuous and talented as his company.

君子居必择居，游必就士。择居所以求士，求士所以辟患也。

《晏子春秋·内篇杂上》

If a gentleman wishes to find a living place, he must make a good choice in his neighbors; when he embarks upon a journey, he must find someone virtuous and talented as his company. The purpose of choosing good neighbors is to look for virtuous and talented persons, and the purpose of looking for virtuous and talented persons is to keep disasters and ruin at bay.

【注释】

孔子弟子曾参离开齐国时，晏子赠以善言：以木工烤直木弯曲制作车轮为喻，强调矫正邪曲的重要；以玉工琢磨璞玉使成为传国之宝为喻，强调修养自身的重要。最后又说，君子居住一定选择好环境，出游一定结交贤士，以防止祸患发生。

【译文】

君子居住一定选择好环境，出游一定结交贤士，选择好邻居是为了寻求贤士，寻求贤士是为了躲避祸患。

君子无礼，是庶人也

If a ruler or a man of virtue does not pay attention to etiquette, he is no different from the common man.

君子无礼，是庶人也；庶人无礼，是禽兽也。

《晏子春秋·内篇谏下》

If a ruler or a man of virtue does not pay attention to etiquette, he is no different from the common man. If the common man does not pay attention to etiquette, he is no different from the animals.

【注释】

君子：一指执政者，一指有才德的人。这里和庶人对称，多指统治者和贵族男子。《尚书·酒诰》："越庶伯君子。"传："众伯君子长官大夫统庶士有正者。"《诗经·魏风·伐檀》："彼君子兮，不素餐兮。"庶人：众人，一般人。泛指无官爵的平民百姓。《论语·季氏》："天下有道，则庶人不议。"

【译文】

执政者或有才德的人没有礼仪，就和一般人没什么区别了；一般人没有礼仪，就和禽兽没什么区别了。

君子有力于民则进爵禄，不辞
富贵

    If a gentleman can serve the people, he can take office and enjoy a wealthy life of ease.

君子有力于民则进爵禄，不辞富贵；无力于民而旅食，不厌贫贱。

《晏子春秋·内篇问下》

If a gentleman can serve the people, he can take office and enjoy a wealthy life of ease. If he cannot serve the people, he should leave office and get used to a hard life of poverty.

【注释】

面对齐庄公的无礼行为，晏子与之争论，因谏言不被采纳，晏子辞官而东耕于海滨。临行说了上面的话。果然几年之后，齐国内乱，庄公亦遭大夫崔杼所杀。有力于民：有为百姓尽力的机会。旅食：跟众人吃一样的饭食。旅，众。《左传·昭公三年》："敢烦里旅。"注："旅，众也。"

【译文】

君子有机会为百姓服务就做官领俸禄，并不拒绝富贵；不能为百姓服务就辞官做平民，安于贫贱。

君子之事君也，进不失忠，退不失行

If a gentleman serves his monarch, he should maintain his loyalty to his position and keep his upright character when not in office.

君子之事君也，进不失忠，退不失行。不苟合以隐忠，可谓不失忠；不持利以伤廉，可谓不失行。

《晏子春秋·内篇问下》

If a gentleman serves his monarch, he should maintain his loyalty to his position and keep his upright character when not in office. If he does not indiscriminatively agree with the monarch at the expense of his honor, it can be said that he is loyal. If he does not seek personal gain at the expense of his integrity, it can be said that he has kept his upright character.

【注释】

晋国大夫叔向〔羊舌肸（xī），又称叔肸，字叔向〕问君子如何侍奉君主，晏子说了上面的话。**苟合：**苟且附合，随便附合。《易·序卦》："物不可以苟合而已，故受之以贲。"

【译文】

君子侍奉君主，当官不失掉忠诚，不当官不失掉操行。不苟且求容以致隐藏忠诚，这可以说是不失掉忠诚；不谋私利以致损害廉洁，这可以说是不失掉操行。

乐贤而哀不肖，守国之本也

Loving the virtuous and capable and being sympathetic to the common people is the foundation of governing a country.

乐贤而哀不肖，守国之本也。今君爱老，而恩无所不逮，治国之本也。

《晏子春秋·内篇杂上》

Loving the virtuous and capable and being sympathetic to the common people is the foundation of governing a country. Now you show mercy to the elderly and extend your care to all people, it shows that you understand the foundation of administrating the country.

【注释】

齐景公怜悯面有饥饿之色的负薪老人，晏子称赞说："君主可怜老年人，因而恩德遍及所有的人，这是治理国家的根本。"**不肖**：品行不好。**逮**：及，到。

【译文】

（君主）喜欢贤德的人同时怜悯品行一般的人，这是掌管国政的根本。现在您（齐景公）爱护老年人，同时把恩惠遍及所有的人，这是治理国家的根本。

礼者，所以御民也；辔者，所以御马也

Etiquette is used to govern the people as the rein is used to tame the horse.

礼者，所以御民也；辔者，所以御马也。无礼而能治国家者，婴未之闻也。

《晏子春秋·内篇谏下》

Etiquette is used to govern the people as the rein is used to tame the horse. I have never heard that a country can be administrated without the use of etiquette.

【注释】

齐景公崇尚勇士，晏子指出，礼才是治理国家最重要的，不可或缺的。没有礼，就不能治理国家。御：治理，统治。《尚书·大禹谟》："御众以宽。"《国语·周语下》："百官御事。"驾驭车马也称御。辔（pèi）：马缰绳。

【译文】

礼仪，是用来治理百姓的；缰绳，是用来驾驭马匹的。没有礼仪却能治理好国家，我（指晏子）没有听说过。

廉者，政之本也

Being honest and free from corruption is the foundation of good political governance.

廉者，政之本也；让者，德之主也。

《晏子春秋·内篇杂下》

Being honest and free from corruption is the foundation of good political governance; being modest is the most important of the virtues.

【注释】

晏子认为，廉洁是政治的根本，谦让是道德的主体，为官积蓄财产必生灾祸，遵守道义才能保全自身。"且分争者不胜其祸，辞让者不失其福。" **本**：事物的根基或主体。《论语·学而》："君子务本。"《商君书·定分》："法令者，民之命也，为治之本也，所以备民也。" **主**：根本。《易·系辞上》："言行君子之枢机，枢机之发，荣辱之主也。"

【译文】

廉洁是政治的根本，谦让是道德的主体。

明君居上，寡其官而多其行，拙
于文而工于事

Wise monarchs do not create too many positions,
they expect their officials to work with high efficiency.
They do not pursue ornate appearances, but are practical and unpretentious in all their actions

明君居上，寡其官而多其行，拙于文而工于事。言不中不言，行不法不为也。

《晏子春秋·内篇问上》

Wise monarchs do not create too many positions, they expect their official to work with high efficiency. They do not pursue ornate appearances, but are practical and unpretentious in all their actions. They do not speak improper words and do not commit illegal acts.

【注释】

寡其官：设置的官职少。行：行动。《论语·公冶长》："今吾于人也，听其言而观其行。"文：文彩。《礼记·乐记》："五色成文而不乱。"中：不偏不倚，无过不及。《论语·子路》："不得中行而与之，必也狂狷乎！"

【译文】

英明君主居上位，设置官职少，办事效率高。不讲究外表华丽，擅长做实事。不正确的话不说，不合法的事不做。

明君居上，无忠而不信，无信而不忠者

The ministers who are trusted by a wise monarch are faithful, and those who are not trusted are not faithful.

明君居上，无忠而不信，无信而不忠者。是故君臣同欲，而百姓无怨也。

《晏子春秋·内篇问上》

The ministers who are trusted by a wise monarch are faithful, and those who are not trusted are not faithful. When the monarch and his ministers are thus united and working as one, the people will have no complaints.

【注释】

晏子认为，治理国家管理人民，有三件事值得忧虑：忠臣不受信任；受信任的臣子不忠；君臣离心离德。上：上位，在上者，指君主。《管子·君臣下》："民之制于上，犹草木之制于时也。" **君臣同欲**：君主和臣子想法相同。欲，想要。《论语·述而》："仁远乎哉？我欲仁，斯仁至矣。"

【译文】

英明君主居上位，没有忠臣不受信任，没有受信任的臣子不是忠臣。所以君臣同心同德，百姓就没有怨恨了。

明王不徒立，百姓不虚至

No one can easily become a wise monarch; it is impossible for the people to submit will one who governs them without being given any reason to support him.

明王不徒立，百姓不虚至。

《晏子春秋·内篇谏上》

No one can easily become a wise monarch; it is impossible for the people to submit to one who governs them without being given any reason to support him.

【注释】

齐景公和晏子在淄水边悠闲地观赏着景色。景公叹息说："要是能长期保住国家，并且传位于子孙后代，不是很高兴的事吗？"晏子说："我听说过英明的君主不是随随便便就能当的，老百姓也不是平白无故就来归附的。可是，你以政乱国，不顾百姓死活已经很久了，现在又说保住国家，传给子孙后代，这不是很困难的事吗？"**徒：**副词。空，徒然。《玉台新咏·古诗为焦仲卿妻作》："妾不堪驱使，徒留无所施。"**虚：**徒然，白白地。《汉书·匡衡传》："是以群下更相是非，吏民无所信，臣窃恨国家释乐成之业，而虚为此纷纷也。"

【译文】

圣明的君主不是随随便便就能当的，老百姓也不是平白无故就会来归附的。

明王之任人，谄谀不迩乎左右
A wise monarch will not let flatterers accompany him.

明王之任人，谄谀不迩乎左右，阿党不治乎本朝。

《晏子春秋·内篇问上》

A wise monarch will not let flatterers accompany him, and will not offer court positions to persons who collude for personal gain.

【注释】

任：任用。《尚书·大禹谟》："任贤勿贰。" 谄谀：阿谀谄媚。《荀子·修身》："以不善先人者谓之谄，以不善和（hè）人者谓之谀。" 迩：近。《诗经·周南·汝坟》："虽则如毁，父母孔迩。"注："迩，近也。"

【译文】

英明的君主任用人才，不让阿谀谄媚者留在身边，不让结党营私的人在朝为官。

能愛邦內之民者，能服境外之不善

The monarch who loves the people in his kingdom has the power to win over the villains of other kingdoms.

能爱邦内之民者，能服境外之不善；重士民之死力者，能禁暴国之邪逆；听赁贤者，能威诸侯；安仁义而乐利世者，能服天下。

《晏子春秋·内篇问上》

The monarch who loves the people in his kingdom has the power to win over the villains of other kingdoms. By valuing his fierce fighters he can stop invasions from cruel neighbors. By using his virtuous and capable subjects he can deter the dukes. By carrying out benevolent governance and loving those who benefit the kingdom he can obtain the support of all people.

【注释】

齐庄公认为威服天下靠的是时机，晏子说靠的是行为。邦：指诸侯国。不善：没有道德的人。不好的人。《论语·子路》："不如乡人之善者好之，其不善者恶之。"士民：古代四民中学道艺或习武勇的人。《管子·五辅》："其士民贵武勇而贱得利。"《穀梁传·成公六年》："古者有四民：有士民，有商民，有农民，有工民。"注："士民，学习道艺者。"死力：必死之力，最大的力量。《六韬·龙韬·立将》："如此则士众必尽死力。"听赁贤者：听信任用贤德之人的人。赁，任用。

【译文】

国君能爱护自己的百姓，也就能使其他诸侯国的恶人归服；看重学道习武之人的必死之力，就能制止凶残国家的侵犯；听信任用贤德之人，就能在诸侯中树立威信；施行仁爱和正义并且以有利社会为乐，就能使天下人归服。

其在朝，君语及之，即危言

**While serving the court, Yan Zi would always reply
to the king's enquiries seriously and honestly.**

其在朝，君语及之，即危言；语不及之，即危行。

《史记·管晏列传》

While serving the court, Yan Zi would always reply to the king's enquiries seriously and honestly. When the king would not ask for his opinion, he would act on the king's behalf in an honest manner.

【注释】

危言：直言。《论语·宪问》："子曰：'邦有道，危言危行。'"《后汉书·党锢传》："又渤海公族进阶，扶风魏齐卿，并危言深论，不隐豪强。"注："危言，谓不畏危难而直言也。"危行：正直的行为。《论语·宪问》："邦有道，危言危行；邦无道，危行言孙。"

【译文】

他（晏子）在朝廷，君主有话问他，他就严肃且直接了当地回答；君主不向他问话，他就正直地行事。

其政任贤，其行爱民

The wise monarch employs virtuous and capable persons, cares for the people of his kingdom.

其政任贤，其行爱民。其取下节，其自养俭。

《晏子春秋·内篇问上》

The wise monarch employs virtuous and capable persons, cares for the people of his kingdom, uses the property of the kingdom moderately, and leads a thrifty and simple life.

【注释】

齐景公问贤明君主如何治理国家。晏子以"任贤""爱民"对。政：政治，政事。《论语·学而》："夫子至于是帮也，必闻其政，求之与？抑与之与？"行：行为。《论语·公冶长》："今吾于人也，听其言而观其行。"节：节制，节约。《墨子·节葬》："葬埋者，人之死利也，夫何独无节于此乎？"

【译文】

（贤明君主治理国家）他们在政治上任用贤人，在行为上爱护百姓。他们取财于民有节制，自己生活俭朴。

轻死以行礼谓之勇

It takes boldness to continue with etiquette regardless of danger.

轻死以行礼谓之勇，诛暴不避强谓之力。故勇力之立也，以行其礼义也。

《晏子春秋·内篇谏上》

It takes boldness to continue with etiquette regardless of danger. It takes force to kill despots without being afraid of the rich and the influential. So the purpose of using boldness and force is to continue etiquette.

【注释】

齐庄公崇尚勇力不实行礼义。问晏子曰："古者亦有徒以勇力立于世者乎？"晏子说了上面的话作为回答。勇：勇敢，大胆。《管子·法法》："上好勇则民轻死。"力：威力。《商君书·开塞》："汤武致强，而征诸侯，服其力也。"勇力：果敢有力。《左传·襄公二十二年》："君恃勇力以伐盟主。"《孙膑兵法·善者》："士有勇力而不得以为强。"

【译文】

奋不顾身实行礼义叫做勇，诛伐凶暴不避豪强叫做力。所以果敢有力的树立，只是为了实行礼义罢了。

任大臣无多责焉，使迩臣无求
嬖焉

If the monarch does not demand perfection when appointing ministers, does not choose his favorites to be close advisers . . .

任大臣无多责焉，使迩臣无求嬖焉。无以嗜欲贫其家，无信谗人伤其心。家不外求而足，事君不因人而进。则臣和矣。

《晏子春秋·内篇问上》

If the monarch does not demand perfection when appointing ministers, does not choose his favorites to be close advisers, does not make ministers poor for his personal gain, and does not grieve his ministers by believing slander, his courtiers will live comfortably without taking bribes and will not be promoted due to personal relationships. In this way the monarch and his courtiers will have prosperous and amicable relations with each other.

【注释】

齐景公问晏子："怎么做才能使君臣和谐，人民亲附？"晏子说了上面的话。迩臣：近臣，君主身边的侍从。迩，近。《诗经·周南·汝坟》："虽则如毁，父母孔迩。"注："迩，近也。"嬖（bì）：宠爱。《史记·周本纪》："幽王嬖爱褒姒。"

【译文】

任用大臣不求全责备，使用近臣不挑选自己宠爱的人。不因自己私欲而使臣子贫困，不听信谗言使臣子伤心。大臣们不求外财而能生活充足，他们被提拔不是靠关系。这样君臣就算和谐了。

任人之长，不强其短

If we want to utilize someone's merits, we should discount his demerits.

任人之长，不强其短；任人之工，不强其拙。

《晏子春秋·内篇问上》

If we want to utilize someone's merits, we should discount his demerits. If we want someone to do what he is good at, we should not force him to do what he is not good at.

【注释】

强（qiǎng）：勉强。《孟子·滕文公下》："强而后可。"工：擅长。《韩非子·五蠹》："工文学者非所用，用之则乱法。"

【译文】

任用人的长处，不勉强任用他的短处；任用人做擅长的事，不勉强他做不擅长的事。

上离德行，民轻赏罚

If the monarch does not follow moral standards, the people will belittle both the rewards and punishments he metes out.

上离德行，民轻赏罚，失所以为国矣。

《晏子春秋·内篇谏上》

If the monarch does not follow moral standards, the people will belittle both the rewards and punishments he metes out. The monarch will then lose his way in the administration of the country.

【注释】

德行：道德，品行。《易·节》："君子以制数度，议德行。"疏："德行谓人才堪任之优劣。"赏罚：奖赏有功，处罚有过。《荀子·富国》："赏行罚威，则贤者可得而进也，不肖者可得而退也，能不能可得而官也。"故说赏罚为治国之术。

【译文】

君主违背道德品行，老百姓就不重视奖赏和处罚，这就丧失了治理国家的方法。

上无骄行，下无谄德

The monarch has no arrogant behaviors, and courtiers are free from flattery . . .

上无骄行，下无谄德。上无私义，下无窃权。上无朽蠹之藏，下无冻馁之民。

《晏子春秋·内篇问上》

（In a country governed by a wise monarch），the monarch has no arrogant behaviors，and courtiers are free from flattery；the monarch is selfless，and courtiers do not overstep their authority；the monarch does not collect superfluous wealth，and his people do not suffer from cold and hunger.

【注释】

景公问："贤明君主如何治理国家？"晏子说了上面的话。**骄行**：傲慢的品行。骄，高傲，傲慢。《论语·学而》："贫而无谄，富而无骄。"**谄德**：谄媚的德行。**私义**：自私的道义。私，凡属于一己者皆曰私。《诗经·小雅·大田》："雨我公田，遂及我私。"**窃权**：超越本人职位而行权。**朽蠹**（dù）：腐烂和虫蛀。《左传·昭公三年》："民参其力，二入于公，而衣食其一。公聚朽蠹，而三老冻馁。"

【译文】

（贤明君主治理国家）君主没有傲慢的行为，臣子没有谄媚的品行。君主没有自私的道义，臣子不干越权的事情。君主不收藏多余的财物，下面没有挨饿受冻的百姓。

赏无功谓之乱，罪不知谓之虐

Granting rewards to a person who has made no contribution to the nation is called an interruption of administration. Penalizing a person who did not know the truth of what they had done is called an act of tyranny.

赏无功谓之乱，罪不知谓之虐。

《晏子春秋·内篇谏下》

Granting rewards to a person who has made no contribution to the nation is called an interruption of administration. Penalizing a person who did not know the truth of what they had done is called an act of tyranny.

【注释】

一个平民无意中吓飞了齐景公要射的鸟，景公就要治其罪，晏子进谏说了上面的话。并指责景公"不明先王之制，而无仁义之心是以从欲而轻诛"。乱：扰乱。《韩非子·五蠹》："儒以文乱法。"罪：治罪，处罚。《尚书·泰誓上》："罪人以族，官人以世。"虐：残暴，侵害。《尚书·汤诰》："夏王灭德作威，以敷虐于尔万方百姓。"

【译文】

赏赐没有功劳的人，叫做乱政；惩罚不了解实情的人，叫做暴虐。

圣人千虑，必有一失；愚人千虑，必有一得

Even a wise man may sometimes make a mistake;
even a fool may sometimes have a good idea.

圣人千虑，必有一失；愚人千虑，必有一得。

《晏子春秋·内篇杂下》

Even a wise man may sometimes make a mistake; even a fool may sometimes have a good idea.

【注释】

齐景公厚赐晏子财物，晏子拒绝。景公说，从前我们的先君桓公把五百社的人口和土地封给管仲，管仲没有推辞，接受了。您为什么就不能接受呢？晏子说，智者千虑，必有一失；愚者千虑，必有一得。管仲的千虑之失，就是我的千虑之得吧！

虑：思考，谋划。《商君书·更法》："君亟定变法之虑，殆无顾天下之议之也。"

【译文】

聪明人考虑问题，也会有疏漏的地方，愚钝平凡的人考虑问题，也会有可取的地方。

食鱼无反，毋尽民力乎

Not trying to exhaust the manpower is just like eating one side of a fish without turning it over.

食鱼无反，毋尽民力乎！勿乘驽马，则无置不肖于侧乎！

《晏子春秋·内篇杂上》

Not trying to exhaust the manpower is just like eating one side of a fish without turning it over. Inferior horses cannot be used as mounts, that is to say the monarch should not use persons who are not virtuous and capable.

【注释】

齐景公在外游玩得一铜壶，内刻"食鱼无反，勿乘驽马"八个字。景公解说：吃鱼只吃一面，不翻过来吃另一面，是厌恶它的腥味；出门不乘劣等马，是厌恶它跑不快。晏子回答说："不能这样解释。"于是说了上面的话。**驽马**：能力低下的马。《礼记·杂记下》："孔子曰：凶年则乘驽马，祀以下牲。"注："驽马，六种最下者。"六马指种马、戎马、齐马、道马、田马、驽马。

【译文】

吃鱼只吃一面，不翻过来吃另一面，是说不能把民力用尽啊！出门不乘坐劣等马，是说君主身边不能安置不贤德的人啊！

疏者有罪，戚者治之

If those who are close are assigned to punish the distant who commit crimes . . .

146

疏者有罪，戚者治之；贱者有罪，贵者治之；君者罪于民，谁将治之？

《晏子春秋·内篇谏上》

If those who are close are assigned to punish the distant who commit crimes; if the nobles punish the poor who commit crimes, then who will punish the monarchs who commit crimes?

【注释】

齐景公说："只有百姓得罪君主，哪里有君主得罪百姓的呢？"晏子说了上面的话后又说："我冒昧地问一句：夏桀和商纣得罪了百姓，他们是被君主杀的呢，还是被百姓杀的呢？"晏子的意思是提醒齐景公"无得罪于民"。

【译文】

疏远的人有罪，亲近者去治理他们；低贱的人有罪，尊贵者去治理他们；君主得罪了百姓，将由谁处治他呢？

四海之内，社稷之中，粒食之
民，一意同欲

When all men unite and work as one . . .

四海之内，社稷之中，粒食之
民，一意同欲，若夫私家之政。

《晏子春秋·内篇问上》

When all men unite and work as one, state issues will
be conducted just as family affairs are managed.

【注释】

晏子说古代圣明君主"生有厚利，死有遗教"，他们的政治受到万民拥戴。粒
食：谓以谷物为食。《礼记·王制》："北方曰狄，衣羽毛、穴居，有不粒食者矣。"
疏："地气寒少五谷，故有不粒食者。"粒，谷米之粒。《孟子·滕文公上》："乐岁，
粒米狼戾。"注："粒米，粟米之粒也。"一意同欲：同心同德的意思。

【译文】

普天之下，全国之中，所有的人都同心同德，对待
国事像对待家事一样尽心尽力。

遂欲满求，不顾细民，非存之
道也

For a monarch to constantly try to satisfy his personal desires regardless of the lives of the common people is not the right way to govern a country.

遂欲满求，不顾细民，非存之道也。

《晏子春秋·内篇谏下》

For a monarch to constantly try to satisfy his personal desires regardless of the lives of the common people is not the right way to govern a country.

【注释】

晏子批评齐景公广建宫室，侵夺民居；修建台榭，毁人坟墓，让生者不得安居，死者不得安葬。并指出这不是为君之道。**遂欲满求**：极力满足私欲。遂，顺，又言如意。《国语·周语下》："节之鼓而行之，以遂八风。"注："遂，犹顺也。"**细民**：小民，平民。《韩非子·和氏》："当今之世，大臣贪重，细民安乱，甚于秦楚之俗。"**存**：保全。《礼记·月令》仲春之月："养幼少，存诸孤。"

【译文】

君主极力满足私欲，不顾百姓死活，这不是治理国家的正确办法。

所谓和者，君甘则臣酸

We can take the flavors as an illustrative example of the relationship between the monarch and his courtiers. If the monarch is sweet, his courtiers should be sour.

所谓和者，君甘则臣酸，君淡则臣咸。

《晏子春秋·内篇谏上》

We can take the flavors as an illustrative example of the relationship between the monarch and his courtiers. If the monarch is sweet, his courtiers should be sour. If the monarch is plain, his courtiers should be salty.

【注释】

关于君臣之间和同的问题晏子以调和五味为喻："君甘则臣酸，君淡则臣咸。"意思是臣子不应该一味顺从君主、投其所好，而应进逆耳忠言，匡正君主过失，这才叫谐和。一味顺从君主，从君之好、饰君之过叫同不叫和。和：谐和。《礼记·中庸》："发而皆中节谓之和。"

【译文】

所谓谐和，用调和五味作比方，君主如果是甜，臣下应该是酸；君主如果是淡，臣下应该是咸。

太山之高，非一石也

Just as the Mt. Tai was not formed by one stone ...

太山之高，非一石也，累卑然后高。夫治天下者，非用一士之言也。固有受而不用，恶有拒而不受者哉？

《晏子春秋·内篇谏下》

Just as the Mt. Tai was not formed by one stone but a large number of small stones, it is impossible for the monarch to govern the country by taking the advice of only one person. While the monarch can refuse to use the advice he is given, he should never refuse to listen to it.

【注释】

晏子对齐景公说："治理国家，应该广开言路，集思广益，而不应该闭目塞听。"太山：即泰山。卑：低。受而不用：虽听取意见而不采纳。受，容纳。《易·咸》："君子以虚受人。"

【译文】

高大的泰山，不是一块石头就能让它那么高的，一小块一小块石头累积起来才使它那样高大。治理天下的人，不能只听一个人的意见。固然有听了意见而不采纳的，哪有拒绝倾听意见的呢？

天地四时，和而不失

Just as the heaven, the earth, the ying and yang, and the four seasons rotate harmoniously and accurately . . .

天地四时，和而不失；星辰日月，顺而不乱。德厚行广，配天象时，然后为帝王之君。

《晏子春秋·内篇谏上》

Just as the heaven, the earth, the yin and yang, and the four seasons rotate harmoniously and accurately, and the stars, the sun and the moon move in order, only a man of morality who has an open mind and follows the laws of nature can become a ruler.

【注释】

失：错过，耽误。《尚书·泰誓上》："时哉不可失。"配天：德配于天。《尚书·君奭（shì）》："故殷礼陟配天，多历年所。"象时：与四时相符。

【译文】

天地阴阳四季法则，和谐而不错乱；太阳、月亮和星宿，依次序运行而不混乱。道德淳厚，品行广博，与上天同德，与四季相符，然后才能称帝称王。

通人不华，穷民不怨

（The country is healthy）when the noblemen are not luxurious and the poor have no complaints.

通人不华，穷民不怨。喜乐无美赏，忿怒无美刑。

《晏子春秋·内篇问下》

(The country is healthy) when the noblemen are not luxurious, and the poor have no complaints; when the monarchs do not grant rewards capriciously, nor abuse punishments out of anger.

【注释】

景公问怎样做才能使国家安定。晏子所列举的条件在当时是难以实现的。**通人不华**：显达的人不奢侈。通人，显达之人。华，浮华。汉·王符《潜夫论·实贡》："是以举世多党而用私竞，比质而行趋华。" **羡赏**：滥施赏赐。羡，多余。**羡刑**：滥施刑罚。

【译文】

显达的人不奢侈，穷困的人不怨恨。君主高兴时不滥施赏赐，愤怒时不滥施刑罚。

通则视其所举

The way to judge a man is to watch whom he recommends when his official career prospers.

通则视其所举，穷则视其所
为；富则视其所分，贫则视其所
不取。

《晏子春秋·内篇问上》

The way to judge a man is to watch whom he recommends when his official career prospers, what actions he does not take when his official career falters, whether he shares his wealth with others when he is rich, and whether he seeks ill-gotten gains when he is poor.

【注释】

齐景公问晏子求贤的方法，晏子说了上面关于考察官吏的方法。**通**：官位显达，得志。**穷**：仕途困窘，不得志。《孟子·尽心上》："穷不失义，达不离道。"与此义通。

【译文】

官运通达时看他举荐什么人，仕途困窘时看他不干哪些事；富有时看他是否分钱财给别人，贫穷时看他是否不苟取不义之财。

为臣比周以求进，逾职业防下隐利而求多

If courtiers collude for their promotions, overstep their authority, press hard on the people, seek personal gains insatiably . . .

晏子说

为臣比周以求进，逾职业防下隐利而求多，从君不陈过而求亲，人臣行此三者则废。

《晏子春秋·内篇问上》

If courtiers collude for their promotions, overstep their authority, press hard on the people, seek personal gains insatiably, curry favor with the monarch and do not point out his faults, the monarch should remove them from their positions immediately.

【注释】

齐景公问晏子："臣子做什么事就应该罢免他。"晏子说了上面的话。**比周**：结伙营私。《管子·立政》："群徒比周之说胜，则贤不肖不分。"**隐利**：隐匿私利。隐，隐瞒。《论语·述而》："二三子以为我为隐乎？吾亦无隐乎尔。"**陈过**：匡正过失。陈，上言。《尚书·咸有一德》："伊尹既复政厥辟，将告归，乃陈戒于德。"过，过失。《尚书·大禹谟》："宥过无大，刑故无小。"

【译文】

做臣子的结党营私以求升职；做事超越职权范围，遏制百姓，隐匿私利，贪得无厌；侍奉君主不能匡正其过失，以邀宠幸。臣子做出这三种事就应该罢免他。

为地战者，不能成其王

He who only fights for territory could never become a ruler.

为地战者，不能成其王；为禄仕者，不能正其君。

《晏子春秋·内篇杂上》

He who only fights for territory could never become a ruler. He who only seeks riches is incapable of correcting the ruler's mistaken judgments.

【注释】

晏子认为，为争夺土地而作战的人，不能够成就王霸之业；为得到俸禄而当官的人，不能纠正君主的过失。作为君主，不应该重用禄仕之臣。

【译文】

为争夺土地而打仗的人，不能成就王霸之业；为得到俸禄而当官的人，不能纠正君主的过失。

为君厚藉敛而托之为民

If the monarch were to increase the taxes and claim it was for the good of the people . . .

为君厚藉敛而托之为民，进谗谀而托之用贤，远公正而托之不顺，君行此三者则危。

《晏子春秋·内篇问上》

If the monarch were to increase the taxes and claim it was for the good of the people, appoint flatterers and proclaim them to be men of virtue and talent, become estranged from his upright and faithful courtiers using the excuse that they were disobedient, then the regime would be in danger of collapse.

【注释】

齐景公问晏子："当君主做出什么事就会危及政权？"晏子说了上面的话。藉：借。《战国策·秦策三》："此所谓藉贼兵而赍（jī）盗食者也。"敛：赋税。《孟子·尽心上》："易其田畴，薄其税敛。"

【译文】

当君主加重赋税却托辞说是为了百姓，任用谗佞谄谀之人却托辞说是任用贤人，疏远正直大臣却托辞说这些大臣不能顺从自己，君主行此三种事情政权就危险了。

为君节养其余以顾民，则君尊而
民安

　　If the monarch himself is thrifty and rewards his
people with the excess property in the land, then he shall
be known as honorable and the people will live easily and
in peace.

为君节养其余以顾民，则君尊而民安；为臣忠信而无逾职业，则事治而身荣。

《晏子春秋·内篇问上》

If the monarch himself is thrifty and rewards his people with the excess property in the land, then he shall be known as honorable and the people will live easily and in peace. If the courtiers are honest and faithful and do not overstep their authority, the administration will work efficiently and they themselves will be honored.

【注释】

齐景公问晏子曰："为君身尊民安，为臣事治身荣，难乎，易乎？"晏子回答说："容易。"景公问："应该怎么做？"晏子说了上面的话。顾：照顾，关心。《商君书·修权》："故大臣争于私而不顾其民，则下离上。"

【译文】

作为君主节俭自身，拿出余财来顾及百姓，那么自身就尊贵，人民就安定；作为臣子忠诚守信，办事不超越职权范围，那么政事就能治理好，自身就荣耀。

下无直辞，上有隐恶

If the courtiers make no just pronouncements and upright suggestions, the monarch will face imminent hidden dangers.

下无直辞，上有隐恶；民多讳言，君有骄行。古者明君在上，下多直辞；君上好善，民无讳言。

《晏子春秋·内篇杂上》

If the courtiers make no just pronouncements or upright suggestions, the monarch will face imminent hidden dangers. If the people dare not speak plainly, the monarch will behave insolently and impiously. A wise monarch has courtiers who frequently make just pronouncements and upright suggestions, and if the monarch welcomes good advice, his people will have nothing that they fear to say aloud.

【注释】

齐景公白天披头散发携妇人乘车出宫，被守门人挡驾而返回，为此感到很没有面子，因而不上朝理事。晏子说了上面的话开导景公。隐恶：潜藏的祸患。讳言：忌讳的话。讳，隐讳。《公羊传·闵公元年》："《春秋》为尊者讳，为亲者讳，为贤者讳。"《左传·僖公元年》："讳国恶，礼也。"

【译文】

臣子如果没有正直的言辞，君主就会有隐患；老百姓不敢说忌讳的话，君主就会有骄横的行为。古代英明君主在位，臣子多有正直的言辞；君主喜欢听有益的话，老百姓就没有不敢说的话。

先民而后身

In governing a country, the people's affairs should take precedence over the personal affairs of the monarch.

先民而后身，先施而后诛。

《晏子春秋·内篇问下》

In governing a country, the people's affairs should take precedence over the personal affairs of the monarch, and bestowing rewards should be more important than meting out punishments.

【注释】

晏子出使吴国，吴王问如何能长久地保持国家的威严强大。晏子针对吴王内政不修而妄想称霸的情况提出"先民后身"的政治主张。施：给予。《国语·吴语》："施民所欲，去民所恶。"

【译文】

把人民的事情放在前面，把个人的事情放在后面；把赏赐的事情放在前面，把惩罚的事情放在后面。

刑罚中于法，废罪顺于民

The execution of punishments must meet the requirements of the law. Pardons should be granted following public opinion.

刑罚中于法，废罪顺于民。

《晏子春秋·内篇问上》

The execution of punishments must meet the require-ments of the law. Pardons should be granted following public opinion.

【注释】

晏子说古代圣明君主施行刑罚符合法律，官吏升降顺应民意。因此"贤者处上而不争，不肖者处下而不怒。"中（zhòng）：击中目标。《左传·桓公五年》："祝聃射王，中肩。"废：停止，废除。《老子》第18章："大道废，有仁义。"

【译文】

施行刑罚符合法律，废除罪名顺应民意。

省行者不引其过

A man who can examine himself critically can forgive mistakes in others.

省行者不引其过，察实者不讥其辞。

《晏子春秋·内篇杂上》

A man who can examine himself critically can forgive mistakes in others. A man who can discern the truth will not mock others' words.

【注释】

省（xǐng）：察看。《易·观》："先王以省方观民设教。"行（xíng）：行为。《论语·公冶长》："今吾于人也，听其言而观其行。"察：观察。《易·系辞上》："仰以观于天文，俯以察于地理。"实：真实，同"虚假"相对。《墨子·尚贤中》："此非中实爱我也，假藉而用我也。"讥：谴责，非议。《左传·隐公元年》："段不弟，故不言弟；如二君，故曰克；称郑伯，讥失教也。"

【译文】

能反省自己行为的人就不会抓住他人的过错不放，能核查实际情况的人就不会讥讽他人的言辞。

以亡为行者不足以存君

The man who regards fleeing abroad as a virtue could never defend the monarch.

以亡为行者不足以存君，以死为义者不足以立功。

《晏子春秋·内篇杂上》

The man who regards fleeing abroad as a virtue could never defend the monarch, and the man who regards resorting to death as loyalty could never render the monarch meritorious service.

【注释】

齐庄公不用晏子，收回官爵和食邑，后被大夫崔杼所杀。崔杼杀死齐庄公后又问晏子："你为什么不殉死？"晏子说了上面的话，表达了他既不为无道君主殉死，又反对逃亡国外以自保的态度。

【译文】

把逃亡国外当做好品行的人不足以保住君主，把殉死当做义气的人不足以建立功勋。

意莫高于爱民，行莫厚于乐民

The noblest thought is to cherish the people, and the best conduct wants only to ensure their happiness.

意莫高于爱民，行莫厚于乐民。

《晏子春秋·内篇问下》

The noblest thought is to cherish the people, and the best conduct wants only to ensure their happiness.

【注释】

晋国大夫叔向问晏子曰："意孰为高？行孰为厚？"晏子说了上面的话。叔向又问曰："意孰为下？行孰为贱？"晏子曰："意莫下于刻民，行莫贱于害民也。"意为：思想没有比对人民苛刻更低下的，品行没有比危害人民更卑贱的。**意**：意思。《易·系辞上》："出不尽言，言不尽意。"此处指思想。**乐民**：让人民快乐。

【译文】

思想没有比爱护人民更高尚的，品行没有比让人民快乐更淳厚的。

淫于耳目，不当民务，此圣王之所禁也

Concentrating only on his own pleasure and ignoring the administration of the state is in no way how a wise monarch should behave.

淫于耳目，不当民务，此圣王之所禁也。

《晏子春秋·内篇谏上》

Concentrating only on his own pleasure and ignoring the administration of the state is in no way how a wise monarch should behave.

【注释】

齐景公听信宠妾的话，重赏无功。晏子指出国君不顾人民疾苦，只图耳目享受，不赏贤人而赏无功，这是与人民为敌，有亡国的危险。**淫于耳目**：过分追求耳目享受。淫，过度，过甚。《尚书·大禹谟》："罔淫于逸，罔淫于乐。"《左传·襄公二十九年》："迁而不淫，复而不厌。"注："淫，过荡。"耳目，耳朵和眼睛。《礼记·仲尼燕居》："若无礼，则手足无所错，耳目无所加。"此处指美色和音乐。**当**：任，担任。**务**：事务。

【译文】

过分追求享乐，不理民政事务，这是圣贤君主所不为的。

愚者多悔，不肖者自贤

The men who are foolish are often regretful, and the men who lack virtue often believe themselves to be virtous and right.

愚者多悔，不肖者自贤。溺者不问隧，迷者不问路。

《晏子春秋·内篇杂上》

The men who are foolish are often regretful, and the men who lack virtue often believe themselves to be virtuous and right. The reason a man drowns is because he does not ask the right road through the water, and the reason a man loses his way is because he does not ask the correct path to take.

【注释】

鲁昭公失国后出逃齐国，说起失国的原因也很在理，齐景公觉得他的悔恨之言说得很好，并认为他返回鲁国后可以成为圣贤君主。晏子则认为，愚蠢的人好后悔，不肖之人总认为自己好。溺水的人是因为不询问水中可以趟过的道路，迷路的人是因为不打听正确的道路。并说："溺而后问隧，迷而后问路，譬之犹临难而遽铸兵，噎而遽掘井，虽速，亦无及已。"隧：道路。《诗经·大雅·桑柔》："大风有隧，有空大谷。"传："隧，道也。"

【译文】

愚蠢的人总好悔恨，不贤德的人总认为自己贤德。溺水的人是因为不问可以通过的水道，迷路的人是因为不打听正确的道路。

责焉无已，智者有不能给
Even the wise cannot do all things impeccably.

责焉无已，智者有不能给；求焉无餍，天地有不能赡也。

《晏子春秋·内篇问上》

Even the wise cannot do all things impeccably. Even God cannot satisfy a man who is insatiable.

【注释】

无已：不止。已，停止。《诗经·郑风·风雨》："风雨如晦，鸡鸣不已。"给（jǐ）：供应。《左传·僖公四年》："贡之不入，寡君之罪也，敢不共给。"餍（yàn）：满足。《国语·晋语》："君臣上下各餍其私，以纵其回。"注："餍，足也。"赡（shàn）：供给，供养。《汉书·王莽传》："收赡名士，交给将相卿大夫甚众。"

【译文】

无限止地要求做所有的事，聪明人也有不能完成的时候；贪得无厌地求取财物，天地之大也有不能满足他的时候呀。

政尚相利，故下不以相害为行

In governance, advocate mutual benefits, so that people will not do things contrary to their mutual benefits.

政尚相利，故下不以相害为行；
教尚相爱，故民不以相恶为名。

《晏子春秋·内篇问上》

In governance, advocate mutual benefits, so that people will not do things contrary to their mutual interests. In education, advocate fraternity, so that people will not regard hostility as source of good reputation.

【注释】

尚：崇尚，尊崇。《论语·阳货》："君子尚勇乎？"相（xiāng）：共，互相。《易·咸》："柔上而刚下，二气感应以相与。"《韩非子·初见秦》："当是时也，赵氏上下不相亲也，贵贱不相信也。"

【译文】

政治上崇尚互相有利，所以人民不把互相损害当做好品行；教育上崇尚互相友爱，所以人民不把互相厌恶当做好名声。

忠不避死，谏不违罪

An honest and faithful courtier is not afraid of death and is not afraid of punishment when he remonstrates against the monarch's mistakes.

忠不避死，谏不违罪。

《晏子春秋·内篇谏下》

An honest and faithful courtier is not afraid of death and is not afraid of punishment when he remonstrates against the monarch's mistakes.

【注释】

齐景公好游玩打猎，又征发徭役修建大台。晏子劝谏说："春夏征发徭役，使百姓失去耕种的时机，国家就会财政空虚。"并针对景公"及时行乐"的思想说："昔文王不敢盘游于田，故国昌而民安。楚灵王不废乾溪之役，起章华之台，而民叛之。今君不革，将危社稷，而为诸侯笑。"景公从谏，停止修建大台之役。**违**：躲避。《易·乾》："乐则行之，忧则违之。"

【译文】

忠臣不避违死亡，进谏君主不怕获罪。

忠臣不信，一患也

A nation's first hidden danger is the monarch having no trust in his faithful courtiers.

忠臣不信，一患也；信臣不忠，二患也；君臣异心，三患也。

《晏子春秋·内篇问上》

A nation's first hidden danger is the monarch having no trust in his faithful courtiers. Its second hidden danger is the courtiers whom the monarch believes are not faithful. Its third hidden danger is any mutual distrust that exists between the monarch and his courtiers.

【注释】

齐景公问治理国家管理人民有什么事值得忧虑？晏子认为，值得忧虑的事情有三件：忠臣不受信任；受信任的臣子不忠；君臣之间离心离德。

【译文】

忠诚的臣子不受信任，这是第一件值得忧虑的事；受信任的臣子不忠诚，这是第二件值得忧虑的事；君主和臣子不能同心同德，这是第三件值得忧虑的事。

诛暴不避强，替罪不避众

To sentence the despots to death and punish the wicked without fear of offending the rich and the influential . . .

诛暴不避强，替罪不避众，勇力之行也。

《晏子春秋·内篇谏上》

To sentence the despots to death and punish the wicked without fear of offending the rich and the influential are true acts of courage and strength.

【注释】

齐庄公奋乎勇力，不顾于行义。故晏子有此谏。并说："今上无仁义之理，下无替罪诛暴之行，而徒以勇力立于世，则诸侯行之以国危，匹夫行之以家残。"替罪：消灭罪恶。替，废弃。《尚书·旅獒》："无替厥服。"传："使无废其职。"

【译文】

诛伐凶暴不避豪强，消灭罪恶不怕势众，这是真正勇力的行为。

诛不避贵，赏不遗贱

The powerful and influential must be sentenced for violations of the law, just as the common people must not be ignored when rewards are conferred.

诛不避贵，赏不遗贱。

《晏子春秋·内篇问上》

The powerful and influential must be sentenced for violations of the law, just as the common people must not be ignored when rewards are conferred.

【注释】

齐景公问晏子说："古代圣明君主行为如何？"晏子对曰："薄于身而厚于民，约于身而广于世；其处上也，足以明政行教，不以威天下；其取财也，权有无，均贫富，不以养嗜欲；诛不避贵，赏不遗贱。"**避**：回避。《汉书·李广传》："匈奴号曰汉飞将军，避之。"**遗**：遗漏。《韩非子·有度》："刑过不避大臣，赏善不遗匹夫。"

【译文】

诛罚不回避权贵之人，赏赐不遗漏低贱百姓。

从邪害民者有罪，进善举过者有赏

The man who poses harm to the people should be known as a criminal. The man who can advise the monarch to redress his faults wisely should be conferred rewards.

198

从邪害民者有罪，进善举过者有赏。

《晏子春秋·内篇问上》

The man who poses harm to the people should be known as a criminal. The man who can advise the monarch to redress his faults wisely should be conferred rewards.

【注释】

从邪害民：放纵邪僻伤害人民。从（zòng）：放纵。通"纵"。《礼记·曲礼上》："欲不可从。"邪（xié）：不正，邪僻。《尚书·大禹谟》："任贤勿贰，去邪勿疑。"《荀子·劝学》："故君子居必择乡，游必就士，所以防邪僻而近中正也。"

【译文】

放纵邪僻伤害人民的人有罪，向君主进善言能匡正君主过失的人有赏。

左右为社鼠，用事者为猛狗

If the attendants to the monarch were like altar rats and the courtiers like savage dogs . . .

左右为社鼠，用事者为猛狗，主安得无壅，国安能无患乎？

《晏子春秋·内篇问上》

If the attendants to the monarch were like altar rats and the courtiers like savage dogs, how could the monarch not be isolated from outside world, and how could the country be without hidden dangers and not near imminent disasters?

【注释】

社鼠：晏子对寄居在社坛里的老鼠的称呼。老鼠住在社坛里，不能用烟熏，不能用水浇，用以比喻齐景公身边的侍从。猛狗：凶猛的狗。晏子说：有个卖酒的人，酒很好，酒器也很干净，卖酒的标记也很显眼，但酒放酸了也卖不出去。原来他家的狗太凶猛了，谁去买酒就咬谁，这就是酒卖不出去的原因。晏子以猛狗喻景公身边掌权的宠臣。壅：堵塞。《左传·成公十二年》："交赘往来，道路无壅。"

【译文】

君主身边的侍从成为社坛里的鼠，掌权的重臣成为凶猛的恶狗，君主怎么能不被隔绝，国家怎么能没有祸患呢？

责任编辑：陆　瑜
英　　译：薛彧威
封面设计：胡　湖
印刷监制：佟汉冬

图书在版编目（CIP）数据

晏子说：汉英对照／蔡希勤编注．—北京：华语教学出
版社，2011
（老人家说系列）
ISBN 978-7-5138-0158-4

Ⅰ．①晏…　Ⅱ．①蔡…　Ⅲ．①汉语—对外汉语教学—
自学参考资料②先秦哲学—汉、英　Ⅳ．①H195.4②B220

中国版本图书馆 CIP 数据核字（2011）第 211634 号

老人家说·晏子说

蔡希勤　编注

*

ⓒ华语教学出版社
华语教学出版社出版
（中国北京百万庄大街 24 号　邮政编码 100037）
电话：(86)10- 68320585　68997826
传真：(86)10- 68997826　68326333
网址：www.sinolingua.com.cn
电子信箱：hyjx@sinolingua.com.cn
北京市松源印刷有限公司印刷
2012 年（大 32 开）第 1 版
（汉英）
ISBN 978-7-5138-0158-4
定价：35.00 元

• 图书推荐 •
Highlights

"老人家说" 系列
Wise Men Talking Series

汉英 Chinese–English edition

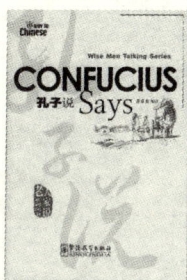

孔子说
Confucius Says
ISBN 9787802002111
201pp,145×210mm
¥29.80

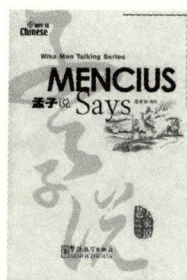

老子说
Lao Zi Says
ISBN 9787802002159
201pp,145×210mm
¥29.80

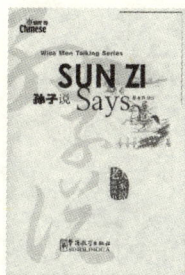

孟子说
Mencius Says
ISBN 9787802002128
201pp,145×210mm
¥29.80

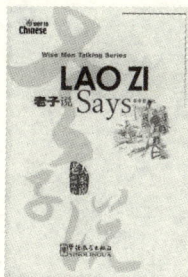

孙子说
Sun Zi Says
ISBN 9787802002142
201pp,145×210mm
¥29.80

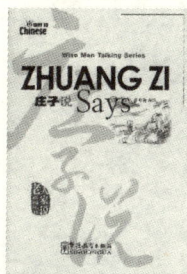

庄子说
Zhuang Zi Says
ISBN 9787802002135
201pp,145×210mm
¥29.80

For more information, visit us at www.sinolingua.com.cn
E–mail:hyjx@sinolingua.com.cn,　**Tel**:0086–10–68320585,68997826

"老人家说" 系列
Wise Men Talking Series
汉英 Chinese–English edition

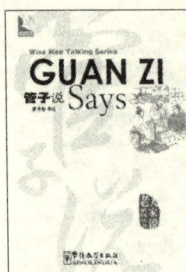

管子说
Guan Zi Says
ISBN 9787513801447
201pp,145×210mm
¥35.00

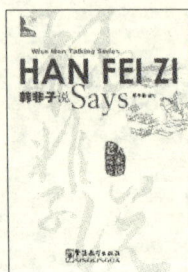

墨子说
Mo Zi Says
ISBN 9787513801454
201pp,145×210mm
¥35.00

韩非子说
Han Fei Zi Says
ISBN 9787513801430
201pp,145×210mm
¥35.00

荀子说
Xun Zi Says
ISBN 9787513801423
201pp,145×210mm
¥35.00

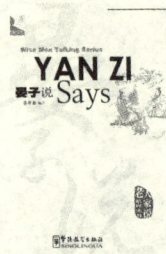

晏子说
Yan Zi Says
ISBN 9787513801584
201pp,145×210mm
¥35.00

For more information, visit us at www.sinolingua.com.cn

E–mail:hyjx@sinolingua.com.cn,　**Tel**:0086–10–68320585,68997826